Housing Research Re

Ba

Models of Practice in Housing Advice

Jo Dean, Robina Goodlad and Ann Rosengard
Centre for Housing Research and Urban Studies
University of Glasgow

Department of the Environment

London : The Stationery Office

ISBN 0 11 753341 6

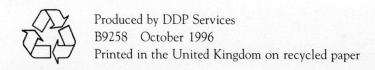
Produced by DDP Services
B9258   October 1996
Printed in the United Kingdom on recycled paper

Contents

List of tables

List of figures

Acknowledgements

We gratefully acknowledge the assistance of many people and organisations in the research for and writing of this report.

Local authorities and their associations, and voluntary sector advice agencies and their federations and parent bodies have helped at all stages in the design and execution of the research. Officers in both sectors helped with completing questionnaires and providing additional information despite many competing pressures on their own time.

Everyone we met in the 19 case study organisations and areas was helpful and hospitable. This type of research could never be done without their assistance.

Juliet Mountford and Louise Dominian of the Department of the Environment have been particularly helpful and supportive throughout. Nile Istephan, Helen Kay and Maeve Wilson assisted with telephone interviewing and data input. Finally, Mary Coleman and Karen Robertson provided secretarial assistance of a very high standard.

1 Summary

1.1 This report is based on research commissioned by the Department of the Environment with the aims of establishing the variety of patterns of housing advice services and identifying innovative practice. The research sought to assess the benefits of different models of advice provision in the local authority and voluntary sectors. The research arose from Government proposals to introduce legislation to place a duty on local authorities to secure the provision of housing advice services to assist people in finding accommodation and to prevent homelessness. (2.2 - 2.6)

1.2 Advice services in the local authority and voluntary sectors have expanded since the 1970s, and since 1980 housing advice services have grown as a result of the social and economic change, and developments in social and housing policies. The growth in homelessness in the 1980s led to a renewed interest in the role advice could play in preventing and alleviating homelessness. (2.7 - 2.30)

1.3 This report is based on results from two surveys, 19 case studies, and an initial review involving interviews with national, regional, and local agencies. A telephone survey of a sample of local authorities achieved 106 replies, and 148 voluntary organisations responded in a postal survey. (2.31 - 2.35)

Housing Advice Services

1.4 Four objectives in housing advice provision were apparent: to ensure clients were aware of their rights and obligations as citizens; to feed the knowledge gained in advice work into the policy process; to ensure improvements in the housing circumstances (including homelessness) of clients; and to assist the efficient operation of the housing market in the private and public sectors. Voluntary organisations particularly stressed the third of these, and some, along with local authorities, also emphasised that citizens should know their rights and obligations. (3.2 - 3.22)

1.5 Three organisational forms of dedicated housing advice service can be identified in local government: centres separate from the housing department; advice sections within the housing department; and advice staff within a section with wider responsibilities. Other authorities include housing advice in the job descriptions of staff with other duties, including duties in relation to homelessness legislation. (3.23 - 3.27)

1.6 Voluntary sector advice agencies include housing aid centres, other specialist agencies, particularly law centres, and general advice agencies, particularly Citizens Advice Bureaux. Other voluntary organisations with a wider or specialist welfare role may also provide housing advice services as part of that role. Dedicated advice services in local authorities and voluntary housing aid centres provide advice on a wider range of housing problems than other agencies. (3.28 - 3.34)

1.7 Around the same proportions of voluntary organisations as local authorities provided types of advice ranging from straightforward information to counselling. However, voluntary organisations are much more likely than local authorities to advocate on behalf of clients. (3.35 - 3.44)

Patterns of provision

1.8 Almost three quarters of London boroughs but fewer than one third of district councils have dedicated advice staff. Advice sections within housing departments are the most common form of dedicated advice service. Many authorities see a close affinity between advice and private sector services. Very few authorities have contracted the

1

provision of housing advice to other agencies, though there is growing interest in the idea. (4.5 - 4.9)

1.9   The majority of local authorities fulfil their duty to offer advice and assistance to people who are found to be homeless but not in priority need, or to be intentionally homeless, through homelessness units. Only one in ten does so through an advice service or centre. (4.10 - 4.25)

1.10   Housing aid centres in the voluntary sector mainly belong to the Shelter or CHAS networks which together contain 49 centres. Law centres are based mainly in large urban areas, and CABx are found in almost every local authority area. Social welfare agencies include those providing services to homeless people and other particular client groups, and some housing associations. In both sectors, secondary services such as training may be restricted by the demands of casework. The overall pattern of provision varies from one local authority area to another, with more sparsely populated areas showing less developed organisational structures for housing advice. (4.25 - 4.39)

Clients

1.11   Statutory and voluntary sector housing advice services focus particularly on the most vulnerable in social and economic terms, and especially on homeless people. The overall measurement of provision is hampered by the lack of a common basis for recording enquiries. (5.2 - 5.17) Client groups, apart from homeless people particularly targeted include women with children after relationship breakdown, private tenants, owner occupiers in debt, black and ethnic minority groups, and people with mental health problems, physical disabilities or learning disabilities. (5.18 - 5.48)

1.12   Efforts to maximise accessibility are hampered particularly in the voluntary sector by poorer premises, but enhanced for some by evening and weekend working and outreach services. (5.49 - 5.69)

Networks and collaboration

1.13   Networks, defined as patterns of working relationships and links between individuals and agencies, are crucial to the delivery of effective housing advice services. Networks, at national, regional and local levels, provide formal and informal means of planning and delivering services. Local forums are rarely focused on advice alone, but despite that, most local authorities and voluntary organisations were involved in them. (6.2 - 6.11)

1.14   Few formal policies for collaboration and referral exist, but informal arrangements often exist for referral and consultation processes between statutory, voluntary and private sector agencies in relation to clients, for the relationships between specialist and general advice services, and for the relationship between primary and secondary services. In practice, very high proportions of agencies refer clients and receive referrals. Collaboration also takes place in relation to planning and service delivery, with joint services sometimes resulting. Joint strategic planning remains relatively un-developed. (6.12 - 6.34)

Resources

1.15   Spending patterns and funding sources for housing advice services proved to be hard to research. Local authorities, with the exception of London boroughs, have rarely provided a separate account of the costs and financial benefits associated with housing advice services. Spending has grown in an ad hoc way and is now being scrutinised in a number of authorities concerned to demonstrate value for money. An agreed model for showing the costs and benefits would be useful. (7.2 - 7.3)

1.16   Local authorities' main source of revenue for housing advice services is their general account. This is likely to be the source of funding for their own services and for funding the voluntary sector. Voluntary organisations are mainly able to draw on funds from a variety of statutory and voluntary sources. Charitable donations are an important source of revenue for most, and, for some, central government is also important. But for most, local authority funding is the key to releasing the efforts of staff and volunteers. (7.4 - 7.26)

1.17 Local authorities and voluntary organisations demonstrate a strong commitment to staff development and training, but local authorities are less likely to provide training in advice skills relevant to casework. (7.27 - 7.36)

Monitoring, evaluation and quality

1.18 Monitoring and evaluation systems are not well-developed in local authorities and voluntary organisations. However, some agencies in both sectors had sophisticated systems for performance review and quality assessment. (8.2 - 8.7)

1.19 A majority of local authorities and voluntary organisations collect information about clients' characteristics and problems, but a smaller proportion of local authorities seek feedback on clients' views of the service. Information is not always used for evaluation purposes, and sometimes insufficient information is collected to allow judgements to be made about the achievement of objectives. (8.8 - 8.23)

1.20 Local authorities with dedicated advice sections had gone further than other authorities towards developing a framework for evaluation. Some voluntary organisations had evaluation systems in place, but not all were geared to answering questions about the quality of housing advice provision. Many agencies were anxious to improve present systems of monitoring and evaluation. (8.24 - 8.46)

Models of practice

1.21 Chapter 9 provides guidance about a range of options for the development of housing advice services. It considers the implications of the patterns of housing advice provision reported in the individual chapters, and outlines alternative models for different aspects of housing advice provision. Key action points are provided for developing a local strategy, including: auditing provision; defining roles and purposes; considering clients' needs; developing networks; identifying costs, benefits and resources; and monitoring and evaluation.

2 Introduction

2.1   This introductory chapter is in three parts. It provides a context by outlining the objectives of the research on which this report is based and the policy context within which housing advice services are currently being debated. Finally, it also contains brief details of the methods used in the study.

Research objectives

2.2   In a statement to the House of Commons by the Housing Minister on 18 July 1994 the Government announced its intention of introducing legislation to place a duty on local authorities to secure the provision of housing advisory services to assist people in finding accommodation and to prevent homelessness. This was re-iterated in the Housing Bill published in January 1995.

2.3   These moves followed publication by the Department of the Environment (DoE) of a consultation paper on access to local authority and housing association tenancies in January 1994. This paper stated Ministers' belief that a comprehensive network of housing advice centres should be established, and invited comments on how this might be achieved.[1]

2.4   In June 1995 a White Paper, *Our Future Homes*, re-iterated the commitment to develop advice services and seek Parliament's approval to strengthen the duties of local authorities:

> *Effective advice and assistance to people looking for accommodation can prevent homelessness and ensure people on low incomes who need to live in the private rented sector are well housed. Giving people access to more information about what properties are available at reasonable rents can help to keep down the housing benefit bill.*

> *We intend to strengthen the duties on local authorities to ensure that proper housing advice services are available in their areas, as part of the reform of homelessness legislation. Many local authorities already provide advice services or support services run by the voluntary or private sectors. Developing these services should be high on authorities' list of priorities for the future, as part of their enabling role.[2]*

2.5   In March 1995 the Centre for Housing Research and Urban Studies (CHRUS) at the University of Glasgow was commissioned by the Department of the Environment to establish and describe the existing variation in the delivery of housing advice and to identify innovative practice with a focus on prevention/relief of homelessness and helping people to find accommodation; (and) to assess the benefits of different models of and initiatives in advice provision.

2.6   Three more specific objectives were:

- to assess different models of advice and information services in preventing homelessness and finding accommodation;

---

1. Department of the Environment (1994) *Access to Local Authority and Housing Association Tenancies; A Consultation Paper*, London, HMSO.
2. Department of the Environment and Welsh office (1995) *Our Future Homes: Opportunity Choice Responsibility - The Government's Housing Policies For England and Wales Cm 2901*, London, HMSO.

- to establish the range of different models for delivering housing advice and to identify innovative practice in strategic planning, meeting client needs, service organisation, relationships between agencies, standards and quality, and funding arrangements;

- to assess the strengths and weaknesses of alternative approaches to the delivery of housing advice and information in the context of securing the provision of comprehensive housing advice services.

Policy context

2.7   The background to this study can be usefully presented in three parts, dealing with the development of advice services, developments in housing policy, and recent policy concerns about homelessness. These are outlined here since they provide an historical background to the current provision of housing advice, and a necessary introduction to the key organisations and issues discussed later in this report.

The growth of advice services

2.8   The development of advice services in Britain is usually traced from the establishment of 4,000 citizens advice bureaux (CABx) in the few months after the outbreak of war in 1939.[3] In the 20 years after the war some local authorities did not follow Government advice that they should take over as funders of such services, and the numbers of bureaux declined. In the late 1960s a target of a CAB in every town of 30,000 population was set by the National Association of Citizens Advice Bureaux (NACAB) and largely achieved by 1977.[4] This growth coincided with "a rapid expansion of other kinds of advice centre for housing, consumer affairs and the law.[5] For example, there were about 25 law centres by the end of 1976, only one of which had been established in 1970.

2.9   Comment on this growth of advice services is sparse, and the phenomenon is likely to be as hard to explain as the parallel developments in citizen participation at about the same time. Possible factors may have been:

- the effect of a better educated and more assertive population following the improvements in state education after 1944;

- the growth of an increasingly complex range of social services which arguably required their clients to have access to advice to assist them to meet their needs. (The Beveridge Report had recommended the setting up of a general Advice Bureau in every local Security Office[6]);

- developments in technology combined with a higher standard of living for most people, creating a new need for consumer advice in the growing markets for consumer goods;

- a developing critique of the alleged insensitivity and inadequacy of public services, suggesting that people require knowledge and support to ensure just and equitable treatment;

- a similar critique of some market-based services, as seen, for example, in Rachmanism and in some spectacular company bankruptcies which left consumers out of pocket;

- a growing perception that new social welfare services and benefits introduced after 1945 had not eliminated poverty and disadvantage, combined with a belief that advice services could assist the poorest and weakest to improve their position.

---

3. National Consumer Council (1977) *The Fourth Right of Citizenship: A Review of Local Advice Services*, NCC.
4. National Consumer Council (1977) *The Fourth Right of Citizenship: A Review of Local Advice Services*, NCC.
5. National Consumer Council (1977) *The Fourth Right of Citizenship: A Review of Local Advice Services*, NCC.
6. *Social Insurance and Allied Services Cmnd 6404* (1942) HMSO.

2.10   Since 1980 the growth in demand for housing advice services in particular has had new origins, such as:

–   the growing complexity of the institutional framework of banks, building societies and insurance companies providing housing financial services;

–   the growth in debt arising from unemployment, poverty and vulnerability;

–   the development of care in the community policies which stress the suitability of housing and other services in meeting certain needs;

–   the frequency of changes in welfare rights and the withdrawal of some benefits;

–   the growth of homelessness amongst groups not significantly affected in the past;

–   the increased rate of marital and relationship breakdown.

2.11   The earliest documented voluntary sector housing advice agency was the Catholic Housing Aid Society (CHAS) established in 1956. In 1970 the first two housing advice centres were opened in London, one by a voluntary organisation (SHAC) the other by a local authority (Lambeth). In 1971 the Minister for Housing invited 29 local authorities with special housing difficulties to set up advice centres, aided through the Urban Programme. By 1974, 14 had done so and a total of 83 local authority centres existed, 23 in London and the remaining 60 in the rest of Britain. The number of voluntary centres was unknown.

2.12   Three features of this early growth of centres stand out. First, there appears to have been a large measure of agreement about the objectives of housing aid: to provide assistance to individuals through intensive case work; to find out about local housing needs and whether policy is appropriate; and to "to bring about a more rational use of both public and private housing resources.[7] These objectives sound familiar today, as will be seen in the next chapter.

2.13   However, this broad consensus masked some tension between statutory and voluntary providers, with concerns about potential conflicts between duties owed to clients and to local authorities by local government officers. An early study of seven statutory and six voluntary centres concluded that statutory providers of advice were not as constrained, nor voluntary providers as free to act solely in the interests of their clients as some commentators alleged.[8]

2.14   The third feature of overall provision was the variety.

In terms of size, location, scope and styles or work, and in terms of relationships with the rest of the local authority housing department, individual authorities have opted for very different models for their HACs. Equally, in the voluntary sector there is a wide spectrum with particularly significant differences emerging in the attitudes of different centres towards "pressuring" local authorities either on behalf of individual clients or else with specific policy objectives.[9]

2.15   By 1979 SHAC estimated there were 175 housing aid centres in Britain (109 run by local authorities - 27 in London, 82 elsewhere - and 66 by voluntary organisations). The slowing down in the rate of formation was attributed to three factors: "saturation" in some areas, public spending restraints, and suspicion of housing aid by some councillors and local government officers.[10]

---

7.   Fox, D. (1973) *Housing Aid And Advice*, Department of the Environment, *cited in* Raynsford, N. 'Housing Aid and Advice' p.5 *in Housing* 15(1), Jan. 1979 pp.4-8.
8.   Harloe, M., Minns, R., & Stoker, G. (1976) *Housing Advice Centres*, Shelter / Centre for Environmental Studies.
9.   Raynsford, N. (1979) *Housing Aid and Advice* p.6 *in Housing* 15(1), pp.4-8.
10.   Raynsford, N. (1979) *Housing Aid and Advice*, p.7 *in Housing* 15(1), pp.4-8.

2.16   Evidence about the number and nature of housing aid centres in the 1980s is sparse, but in the early 1990s there were at least 100 local authority centres in England. In 1995, little was known systematically about the pattern of provision, models for provision and effectiveness of specialist housing advice centres, or about the housing role of general advice services (such as CABx) and other specialist advice services (such as law centres). In the mid-1980s local authorities were said to vary greatly in their approach, in some cases providing no advice whatsoever and "rural areas tended to do very badly.[11] In the voluntary sector, also, variations detected included differences in the definitions of "advice" and "assistance", in levels of funding, and in client groups served.

2.17   In 1977 the National Consumer Council proposed a model for advice provision involving neighbourhood "generalist" advice centres supplemented by a wider network of specialist agencies (including housing aid centres). The model provided standards against which provision could be evaluated for staffing; service provision; accessibility; physical access, opening hours and waiting times; and performance review.[12]

Housing policy

2.18   Changes in housing policy at national and local level since 1970 have influenced the development of housing advice services in many ways. The roles of the market and local housing authorities have been particularly important strands in policy.

2.19   The Seebohm Report on social services proposed a new view of the role of housing authorities in 1968 to extend the roles of building new council housing or redeveloping inner city slums which had dominated the post-war years. This more comprehensive role should involve:

> *assisting a family to obtain and keep adequate accommodation, whether it be in the council house sector or not... A local authority should provide a centre for housing advice and guidance...*[13]

2.20   The "comprehensive" housing authority was expected to take a strategic view of housing issues and work with others to implement improvements.[14] After 1979 the emphasis on national policy switched to reducing the local authority's role as provider of housing and increasingly the word "enabling" was used to describe the role. One early 1990s account of the "enabling" role of housing authorities distinguishes six aspects, including providing or securing information and advice.[15]

2.21   Since 1979 the solution to individual housing problems has been seen as likely to lie less in quick access to council housing - though that has remained an important route for many - and more in private renting, housing associations and low cost home ownership. The policy emphasis shifted towards private landlords and housing associations as the key sources of rented housing, with owner occupation as the tenure of choice for the majority.

2.22   The role of the market is also being extended by requiring local authorities to put out to tender the provision of services such as housing management. Although "housing advice" is not included in the list of "defined activities" which must be included in contracts,[16] it has been open to authorities to enter into contracts for the provision of housing advice services.

---

11. National Consumer Council (1986) *Good Advice For All: Guidelines On Standards For Local Advice Services: A Discussion Paper*, National Consumer Council.
12. National Consumer Council (1977) *The Fourth Right of Citizenship: A Review of Local Advice Services*, London NCC.
13. *Report of the Committee on Local Authority and Allied Personal Services (Seebohm report)* (1968), Cmnd 3703, London, HMSO.
14. HSAG (1978) *Organising a Comprehensive Housing Service*, Department of the Environment.
15. Goodlad, R. (1993) *The Housing Authority As Enabler*, Longman / Institute Of Housing.
16. Association of District Councils / Chartered Institute of Housing (1995) *Competition and Local Authority Housing Services: A Guidance Manual*, Association of District Councils / Chartered Institute of Housing.

2.23   Changes in policy have influenced housing advice services. When CHAS was formed in 1956 its early work concentrated on assisting working class families into low cost home ownership. Over the years other opportunities available to people in pressing need were pursued, varying with policy change as well as with local circumstances. Since 1977, the work of housing aid services has involved, *inter alia*, assisting people in relation to homelessness legislation.

Homelessness

2.24   Prior to 1977, voluntary organisations campaigned for new statutory rehousing duties to be laid on housing authorities. Legislation in that year (now Part III Housing Act 1985) created new duties on local authorities to secure accommodation for certain categories of "priority" applicant (broadly families with children and single people with particular needs or vulnerability). Applicants who did not qualify were entitled to advice and assistance. Since 1977 campaigning activity has concentrated on seeking amendments to the legislation and on urging more positive use of discretion in its implementation. Advice providers have used the legislation to assist people, or have sometimes - mainly in the case of voluntary agencies - used their knowledge of the law to challenge decisions taken by housing authorities in particular cases. Any significant change in homelessness legislation is likely to alter the character of the campaigning and case work of housing advice agencies.

2.25   Since 1977 local housing authorities have had specific duties to provide information, advice or assistance to homeless applicants, whether or not the applicant is in priority need. The 1991 Homelessness Code of Guidance which authorities must take into account in carrying out their duties contains a section entitled *Advice and Assistance* which elaborates on the nature of the obligation on housing authorities:

> *Authorities should interview everyone for whom it has a duty to provide advice and should counsel them on the local accommodation options open to them, where appropriate referring them to other specialist agencies.*[17]

2.26   Other factors, apart from the legislative framework, have influenced the work of advice agencies. Foremost amongst these is the growth in homelessness. Leaving aside any possible growth in homelessness arising from housing and social policy changes, demographic, social and economic changes in the 1980s have tended to increase homelessness. Advice agencies have seen a growth in homelessness arising from factors such as marital and relationship breakdown, young people leaving home earlier, the fluctuations in unemployment and interest rates, the closure and contraction of large hostels and other institutions, and the rise in forms of offending and the housing problems of ex-offenders (for example, drug related).

2.27   After 1977 there was a slow, then faster, rise in the number of applicants accepted as homeless under the legislation until 1991, since when there has been a slow decline. The number of acceptances however, does not include non-vulnerable single people who are generally excluded from a right to accommodation, but are entitled to receive "advice and assistance". Some of the growth in homelessness amongst this group in the 1980s was the cause of most public and political concern, for example when young people left home in the provinces to move to London, often for work, but could find nowhere to live.

2.28   Some causes of homelessness posed specific challenges to advice agencies. For example, the growth in youth homelessness was often a challenge for social services as well as housing providers and housing advice agencies. A breakdown in some community care arrangements led to some increase in homelessness amongst the most vulnerable. Problems arising from mental illness or from physical or sexual abuse, for example, had to be taken into account in the provision of housing and other advice.

---

17. Department Of The Environment / Department Of Health / Welsh Office (1991) *Homelessness Code Of Guidance For Local Authorities*, (3rd Ed) HMSO.

2.29 Economic developments, such as the 1988 housing market boom followed by depression coupled with employment insecurity, were reflected in a rise in mortgage arrears and repossessions. Continuing high rates of unemployment confirmed debt as a major precipitator of housing problems. This brought new demands on the skills and knowledge of housing advisers, and the number of money and debt advice services grew.

2.30 Whatever the complex causes of the rise in the 1980s, increasing efforts to prevent or alleviate homelessness became a feature of housing policy by the end of the decade. Advice was seen as one possibly important and cost effective way of preventing homelessness or assisting homeless people to be rehoused. One exponent of this view - the Audit Commission - found that "In just over half of all cases (reported in a survey of local authorities) the provision of housing advice and assistance led to a solution to the client's housing problems.18

Method

2.31 Given the policy context it was considered important to have more systematic information on existing forms and levels of provision of housing advice and on the models of practice that exist. To research these questions fully required in addition some qualitative information.

2.32 This report, therefore, is based on three sources of data:

- a literature review, and interviews with key agencies involved in the provision and development of housing and other advice services: a total of 22 interviews were conducted with 14 national, two regional and six local agencies;

- two surveys: a telephone survey of 128 (one in three) local housing authorities (in which 106 took part), and a postal survey of 407 voluntary sector organisations providing housing advice services in 60 (one in six) local authority areas (to which 148 replied);

- case studies of housing advice provision in ten local authority areas and in nine innovative projects or services.

2.33 The quantitative results are considered a reliable indicator of the national picture of housing advice provision by local authorities. The survey of voluntary organisations produced a poorer response rate and have to be treated with caution, but are considered to provide a broadly representative account of the role of different types of voluntary organisations in housing advice provision. Fuller details of the research method are provided in the Appendix.

2.34 This study did not research consumers' views of advice services systematically, although some contact with consumers took place, and advice agencies were asked about their conduct of such surveys. The experiences and perceptions of consumers have an important part to play in evaluating advice services, and further research would be useful to assist the development of methods for researching them as well as in providing valuable insights into consumers' needs.

2.35 This report provides an account of the results of the programme of work. It is intended to be read by professionals and policy makers interested in the development of housing advice services in England. The central chapters of the report provide results from all the component parts of the research. Chapter 3 considers the interpretations of "housing advice" used in practice, and the forms advice takes; Chapter 4 examines the pattern of provision of housing advice by local authorities and voluntary organisations; Chapter 5 reports who is served and how accessibility is promoted; Chapter 6 looks at the relationships between networks of advice agencies and clients; Chapter 7 considers costs and resources; and Chapter 8 describes the methods advice agencies use to promote quality. A final chapter draws conclusions about the present pattern of advice service provision in England, and provides pointers towards good practice.

---

18. Audit Commission (1989) *Housing The Homeless: The Local Authority Role*, London, HMSO.

3 What are "Housing Advice Services"?

3.1   Any study of the nature and extent of service provision must start by clarifying what service is being examined. This chapter uses evidence about the definitions of "housing advice services" used in practice to illustrate the variety of housing advice services, and the implications of that variety for service delivery, development, resources and evaluation. It therefore provides a necessary preliminary to the description of existing services and the consideration of models for housing advice services which follow in later chapters. Three questions are posed about the nature of housing advice services:

- **What are the objectives or purposes of housing advice services?**

  The nature, costs and effects of advice services cannot be evaluated if the purpose of service provision is not clear.

- **What are the boundaries between housing advice services and other services?**

  The boundaries between housing and other advice services, between housing advice and other housing services, and between housing advice and other social welfare services need to be clarified, before the nature and extent of service provision can be established.

- **What is the meaning of "advice"?**

  Differences between "advice", "aid", "assistance" and "advocacy" have implications for the resources and skills required by advice services. Are all of these to be included in a definition of housing advice?

The purposes of housing advice services

3.2   Public statements by advice services are not always explicit about purposes, but some examples were easily obtained, and local authorities and voluntary organisations were asked about their organisations' objectives in the provision of housing advice in the surveys. Broadly, four strands emerge, called here the **citizenship**, **policy**, **service rights** and **market efficiency** aspects of advice services.

Citizenship

3.3   Voluntary organisations and local authorities, both in significant numbers, saw advice as essential to the exercise of citizenship obligations and rights. For example, the Advice Services Alliance (a federation of national agencies representing independent advice agencies in the voluntary sector) argues that:

> *Without reasonable access to information, advice and representation we are unable to give or get, our dues as citizens.*[1]

3.4   Similarly, NACAB's statement of objectives begins:

> *to ensure that individuals do not suffer through lack of knowledge of their rights and responsibilities or of the services available to them, or through an inability to express their needs effectively...*[2]

---

1. Advice Services Alliance (undated) *The Case for Advice 2,000* (leaflet).
2. NACAB (1994) *Annual Report 1993/4*, NACAB.

3.5   Individual CABx re-iterated this objective; and some other voluntary organisations stated a commitment to ensuring access to advice for all. For example, one law centre wrote of providing "advice and assistance to all users of housing ... regardless of income". Another borough-wide advice centre wrote: "The objects of the centre are to ... (provide) legal advice, assistance, representation and services which (people) could not otherwise obtain through lack of means". But most other voluntary organisations put a different emphasis (see below) at the forefront of their statement of objectives.

3.6   Over eight out of ten local authorities (85%) agreed that ensuring advice is available to citizens is an objective of their organisation (Table 3.1). Officers sometimes stressed that their authority as a whole would wish all citizens to have access to advice, but their housing advice centre or service was targeted on particular disadvantaged groups or tenures, rather than all citizens, whose needs, some knew, were met by other agencies such as CABx. Given the diversity of voluntary organisations surveyed, it was not possible to ask a comparable question, but the statements of objectives supplied by the voluntary sector showed some support for a citizenship view, particularly amongst CABx.

3.7   Agencies which aimed to help all citizens seemed likely to provide advice to all enquirers, consulting other agencies with specialist expertise if necessary, whereas agencies which targeted their services in some way were more likely to refer the client to another agency, perhaps making an appointment for them.

Policy

3.8   NACAB's statement of objectives adds a second **policy** objective which NACAB regard as equally important. Their statement continues:

and equally to exercise a responsible influence on the development of social policies and services, both locally and nationally.[3]

Table 3.1	Objectives held by local authorities in housing advice provision (percentages)			
Objective	**Type of Authority**			**All Authorities**
	London Boroughs	**Metropolitan Councils**	**District Councils**	
Sample number	23	22	59	104
	%	%	%	%
Advice to all citizens	83	96	81	85
Learn about housing conditions and problems	52	59	59	58
Prevent or alleviate homelessness	100	100	97	98
Improve people's housing circumstances	100	91	78	86
Assist smooth running of public or private market	52	50	37	43

Source: *Telephone survey*

3.9   This policy role is often emphasised by agencies in the statutory and voluntary sectors. For example, certain local authorities have responded to a growing problem of mortgage arrears through policy initiatives including liaison with the Council of Mortgage Lenders. Another example is the development of rent deposit schemes.

3.10   This potential role was explored by asking local authorities whether it was their objective to learn more about housing conditions and problems from clients. Nearly six out of ten (58%) of the local authorities agreed it was (Table 3.1). Again, inner London boroughs were less likely than other types of authority to agree, and authorities with a

---

3.   NACAB (1994) *Annual Report 1993/4*, NACAB.

separate housing advice section were more likely than authorities with other organisational arrangements to agree.

3.11   Voluntary organisations varied in how far they stressed this objective. CABx said it was just as important as ensuring citizens knew their rights. An organisation working for and on behalf of those infected or affected by HIV said its objectives included improving housing conditions. A housing aid centre said its objectives included "(addressing) inequalities in choice and opportunity facing individuals and groups... in housing and related fields".

3.12   In the voluntary sector the "policy" role may be carried out through "campaigning" or development work which is administratively separate from advice provision. The work of the large national housing advice agencies, Shelter and CHAS, is structured to distinguish between the two aspects of work: campaigning, including seeking to influence policy, and advice giving. The relationship between them is explicit, however, in this statement by Shelter's housing services director:

> If, say, there are a number of cases from the same building society moving very quickly to repossession, we will tackle this at the policy end, by talking to the society about their practices to see if they will change their policy.[4]

3.13   However, "the business" of housing aid is said to be "preventing homelessness where possible and alleviating the suffering caused by homelessness where not possible.[5] This emphasis on improving the position of the individual client is different from the citizenship and policy purposes of housing advice.

Service rights

3.14   The **service rights** approach places obtaining a remedy for the client at the core of its operation. This objective is held by virtually all the agencies surveyed. All but two local authorities (98%) agreed that they sought to prevent or alleviate homelessness (Table 3.1), and almost nine in ten (86%) agreed that they sought more generally to improve people's housing circumstances. Local authorities emphasise the importance of being prepared to pursue a remedy through, for example, legal action against a private landlord, but also sometimes detect a tension between enforcing the rights of one client and ensuring the continued supply of accommodation, in particular privately rented housing.

3.15   Voluntary organisations also stressed this objective more than any other, as these statements of objectives illustrate:

> to work towards resettlement of men in our care (Salvation Army)

> to offer temporary accommodation and advising women of their options in permanent move on accommodation (a womens aid group)

> to help young people at risk of losing a tenancy to maintain that tenancy (an organisation working to support young homeless people)

> to give the best option available for the client's needs (Indian Workers Association).

3.16   Some voluntary organisations are keen to emphasise these objectives as being more important than simply ensuring that clients have access to information about their rights. They see it as a strength that they are tenacious in seeking to enforce the right to accommodation which they believe every client has, whatever their precise legal entitlement. As a consequence they can feel great frustration when remedies are hard to obtain. The aims of one housing aid centre illustrate this approach:

> (We believe) that every member of our community has the right to a decent, secure home at a price s/he can afford. (This agency) recognises that these standards do not apply to the lives of a significant number of families and individuals. (It) is therefore working to bring about a better housed society, with a particular regard for those in the greatest housing need.

---

4.   Casey, L. (1995) 'Together For London's Aid' in Roof, May, p.12.
5.   Casey, L. (1995) 'Together For London's Aid' in Roof, May, p.12.

3.17   A fourth emphasis, on **market efficiency,** has grown increasingly strong in recent debates about housing advice services. The Audit Commission, for example, sees market efficiency as well as service rights objectives in housing advice:

> *(It) can help to resolve housing problems and prevent homelessness* **without the need to provide a local authority tenancy.**[6] *(our emphasis)*

3.18   This objective is apparent also in the Department of the Environment's Consultation Paper on access to tenancies:

> *Adopting an active role with advice and counselling will help authorities to manage the demand for the stock in their control more effectively... The intention would be to lubricate rather than control the market.*[7]

3.19   The 1995 White Paper, *Our Future Homes*, refers to possible savings on the housing benefit bill, and "helping people to keep their existing homes" and to "steering them towards alternatives"[8] as outcomes of timely advice and assistance.

3.20   An interest in improving access to the market is shown also in the work of some housing departments when they assist prospective tenants with information about private landlords, or offer advice and information to landlords about their obligations and rights. However, fewer than half (43%) agreed it was an objective to assist the smooth running of the market in the public or private sector (Table 3.1). Six out of ten inner London boroughs (60%) agreed it was an objective, while district councils were least likely to agree, with just under four out of ten (37%) confirming it was (Table 3.1).

3.21   In contrast, an emphasis on market efficiency is hard to detect in the statements of objectives provided in the voluntary organisation survey. Arguably this aim is explicit in statements such as "to enable young people to access choices in the housing market", but the emphasis is still on the effect this will have on the client rather than the market.

3.22   Although four purposes of housing advice have been highlighted, in practice these often co-exist in the work of advice agencies. Some agencies place priority on one objective above others, while many others seek to pursue more than one objective simultaneously. Broadly, some voluntary organisations place emphasis on providing information about rights, but more voluntary organisations emphasise the need to secure a good outcome for their clients. Local authorities tended to have multiple aims, with the prevention or alleviation of homelessness as a dominant focus. Some authorities with the best developed services were clear that some possible aims for their service were not pursued, whereas some with poorly developed services were a little unsure. While the objectives do not conflict with each other, there may be times when, for resource or other reasons, all cannot be pursued equally. This typically complex pattern of multiple objectives illustrates the potential difficulty of evaluating services. Since the objectives pursued have implications for the choice of measures, standards or indicators that should be used in evaluation, it is clear that for most agencies, evaluation would not be entirely straightforward or necessarily easy.

Housing advice and other services
Housing advice within housing services

3.23   The second issue considered in this chapter is the boundary between housing advice and other services. "Housing advice services" may be distinguished from other housing services, and from other advice services.

---

6.   Audit Commission (1989) *Housing The Homeless: The Local Authority Role*, London, HMSO.
7.   Department of the Environment (1994) *Access to Local Authority and Housing Association Tenancies; A Consultation Paper*, London, HMSO.
8.   Department of the Environment and Welsh office (1995) *Our Future Homes: Opportunity Choice Responsibility The Government's Housing Policies For England and Wales* Cm 2901, London, HMSO.

Local authorities

3.24 For local authorities, the boundary between housing advice and other services could not be clarified satisfactorily by examining the statutory powers and duties of housing authorities for two reasons. First, these are very limited in relation to housing advice and provide more *powers* than *duties*, a situation which tends to lead to great diversity in the practices of authorities. The key duty to provide advice relates to homelessness (see 4.22). Other duties, for example in relation to tenants' rights, emphasise information provision rather than advice and assistance. And second, local authorities have a number of specific duties and powers to regulate or provide housing services which require advice and information to be provided as part of a service, such as in the administration of improvement and renewal grants, the administration of housing benefit, and the prosecution of private landlords in some circumstances. The administration of the homelessness legislation is a key example, and this study was particularly focused on how the advice needs of homeless people are met. In addition, the study was intended to quantify the extent to which authorities had established dedicated housing advice services and to explore how these related to their other housing services. Overall, local authorities are considered to have adequate statutory powers to provide comprehensive housing advice services, but there has been no such explicit statutory duty, nor any requirement to provide services in any particular organisational form.

3.25 Five organisational forms of provision of housing advice services within local government were identified in the study (Figure 3.1). The first three forms were the most easily identifiable as dedicated advice services. First are advice centres separate from the housing department in their reception and office facilities and in their accountability, for example to a chief executive rather than the housing director (these may or may not use the word "housing" in their title and may or may not provide other advice services). Second, there are housing advice sections (sometimes called centres) within the housing department which were clearly seen as part of the housing department, but had identifiable staffing and management arrangements. The third type of service is provided by staff with a remit only or mainly to provide housing advice, but working within a unit or section with other responsibilities as well. Together these three forms of provision are referred to as "dedicated" housing advice services, and they all indicate a recognition by local authorities that housing advice can be separated in some administrative and staffing sense, from other housing services.

Figure 3.1	Organisational forms of housing advice services in local authorities
Organisational Form	**Relationship to Housing Department**
Separate centre	separate from housing department in reception and office facilities; staff accountable to senior officer other than Housing Director
Separate section	advice section (sometimes called "centre") within housing department, but with own identifiable staff, accountable to Housing Director; reception arrangements vary
Separate staff	identifiable advice staff, working within unit or section with other responsibilities, accountable to Housing Director; reception arrangements as for housing department
Part of staff duties	advice is one of a number of duties within officer's job description; reception arrangements as for housing department
Statutory duties only	advice is provided in relation to statutory duties only (particularly in relation to homeless people)

Source: *Interviews and postal survey*

3.26 Fourth were authorities who included housing advice in the job descriptions of staff with other duties, for example allocations and estate management staff. Fifth, there were authorities in which advice services did not extend beyond statutory duties, particularly in relation to homeless people.

3.27 In practice there may not be a great difference between these categories. For example, staff in the last type of authority may interpret their duties liberally to encompass people with a distant threat of homelessness, and may also provide a case-work service. Here the extent of the advice "service" could be greater than authorities with other organisational forms of service.

Voluntary organisations

3.28 In the voluntary sector it was apparent that several different types of voluntary organisation were providing advice services to people with housing problems. Broadly, two types of voluntary organisation were identified: agencies whose explicit remit is to provide advice (called here *advice agencies*), and agencies which provide advice amongst other social welfare services (called *social welfare agencies* or *services*). In relation to advice agencies, this study had an interest not only in specialist housing aid centres, but also in "generalist" advice agencies, such as CABx, and specialist agencies, such as law centres and money advice centres, whose work may include housing-related cases.

3.29 In relation to social welfare agencies, the possible contribution to the overall provision of advice services by organisations whose functions include advice was apparent, for example in the work of day centres for homeless people and women's refuges. These social welfare organisations are likely to have a target client group or groups, such as homeless people, ex-offenders, or people entitled to community care services. Some housing associations or other non-local authority housing providers can also be seen as social welfare organisations. In practice, however, the distinction between advice agencies and agencies which provide advice as well as other services may not always be clear, as in the example of a service which provides short stay accommodation and counselling about future housing and employment or training options for homeless young people. However, a distinction can usually be drawn between advice agencies, and social welfare agencies which provide advice amongst other services. Agencies of either type may include those established jointly by two or more organisations. Separating these roles and functions provides a ninefold classification, see Figure 3.2.

Figure 3.2	Types of agency providing housing advice		
	Specialist		
	Generalist	**Housing**	**Other**
Advice Agencies (voluntary or statutory)	eg CABx	eg Shelter and CHAS aid centres	eg law centres, disability advice services
Social Welfare organisations (whose work includes housing advice)	eg social services departments, residents' associations	eg housing departments, housing associations	eg Women's Aid, Age Concern, day centres
Private sector organisations	eg solicitors	eg estate agents	eg banks, building societies

Private sector services

3.30 Private sector organisations, such as building societies, banks, estate and accommodation agencies, and solicitors, are not the focus of this study, but their role is acknowledged here and elsewhere in this report. Their advice role is closely associated with their roles as financiers, conveyancers, and property owners' agents, and they have therefore an interest in protecting their own or their clients' assets and interests. This means they may not be seen as necessarily appropriate as advisers in certain circumstances, for example, a tenant in dispute with a landlord who is the agent's client. Also, they are not generally seen as the institutions or professionals who are best placed to serve the advice needs of the most vulnerable, and those who could not afford the charges for some of their services. However, they are seen increasingly as important actors in the local housing market, and, in that, their role as advisers is recognised, particularly since the growth in the incidence of mortgage arrears in the early 1990s. Some of the developing experience of liaison between private, voluntary and public sector agencies is reported in Chapter 6.

Housing and other advice

3.31   There is, in practice, no clear division between housing and other advice. Agencies surveyed were broadly left free to define housing advice as they wanted, but it was evident that all would not do so in the same way. This is particularly apparent in the work of agencies not primarily identified as housing advice agencies. For example, housing is consistently the subject of a significant number of enquiries to "generalist" advice agencies such as CABx, and specialist agencies such as law centres and money advice centres. Similarly in the statutory sector, housing can be an important aspect of the family or individual problems brought to social and health workers, for example, as well as to housing departments. Recognising this is essential, but it does not necessarily make easy the measurement of demand for *housing* advice. Interviewees stressed the complexity and multi-faceted nature of some clients' problems, in which housing, debt, unemployment and marital breakdown, for example, may all be elements, and in which the "presenting" problem - the issue first raised by the client as the problem - may prove to be one of a number of more complex issues to be tackled. Most agencies cannot record all aspects of clients' problems, so housing aspects may go unrecorded at times, or be reported as the main problem when other agencies would define them otherwise.

3.32   This has implications for developing and evaluating housing advice services. It is hard to measure the extent of demand and provision. For example, when NACAB reports that housing issues accounted for ten per cent (761,000) of enquiries handled in 1993/4, it is possible that housing was also an element in the 1.77 million enquiries concerned with "debt and consumer" issues and in the 2.5 million enquiries on social security and family and personal issues.[9] People's problems do not fall into the neat administrative categories that advice agencies may use as simplifying devices. There is no standard classification in use for enquiries brought to advice agencies; nor is there any standard method for adopting one. Even the clearest, most efficient classification system would be unlikely to provide a consistently applied, true measure of demand for housing advice, since some problems with housing dimensions would inevitably be classified under other headings. This suggests caution is required in interpreting the number of "housing" enquiries reported by agencies in an area as a true measure of demand, even if systems were improved and standardised.

Nature of housing problems

3.33   Advice may be provided on a number of different aspects of housing. Broadly these might be concerned with access to accommodation, or with use of the existing home. Local authorities provide advice on a wide range of aspects of access and use (Table 3.2). Furnishing schemes and rent deposit schemes were the only two aspects on which fewer than four out of five authorities overall provided advice - reflecting the absence of these facilities in many areas. Authorities with dedicated advice services provided advice consistently on more aspects of housing than authorities without such services.

---

9.   NACAB (1994) *Annual Report 1993/4*, NACAB.

Table 3.2	Advice provided by local authorities on different aspects of housing (percentages)			
Aspects of Housing	**Type of Authority**			**All Authorities**
	London Boroughs	Metropolitan Councils	District Councils	
Sample number	20	21	61	102
	%	%	%	%
Security of tenure	100	100	100	100
Where else to get help	100	100	98	99
How to register, council waiting list	100	100	95	97
Protection from eviction or harassment	100	100	95	97
How to register, housing association/co-operative lists	90	100	98	97
Welfare rights and benefits	90	95	92	92
Resolution of disputes	90	95	90	91
Aids and adaptations	75	95	90	88
B&B hotels/hostels	100	81	82	85
Availability of supported accommodation	85	95	82	85
Money, arrears and debt advice	80	100	79	83
Accommodation agencies	100	57	82	80
Vacancies in the private sector	80	76	80	79
Furnishing schemes	65	81	53	61
Rent deposit schemes	70	33	62	58

Source: *Telephone survey*

3.34 Voluntary organisations also provide advice on a wide range of housing problems (Table 3.3). At least two thirds of housing aid centres provide advice on all but two types of problem: aids and adaptations, and resolution of disputes. These are both considered very specialist fields, and, in the case of aids and adaptations, advice is closely associated with statutory provision. There were several aspects of housing on which more than four in five of the voluntary organisations provided advice - security of tenure, how to register on council and housing association lists, money, welfare rights, and protection from eviction. Other voluntary organisations did not provide housing advice on such a wide range of topics as specialist housing aid centres, however. Vacancies in the private sector stands out, in particular, as a topic on which fewer than half provided advice. There are two possible reasons why this figure is so low. First, information on vacancies can be hard to obtain or keep up to date and some landlords prefer to publicise vacancies by word of mouth. Second, some voluntary organisations are unconvinced that the private rented sector is an appropriate option for their client group or are wary in case provision of information is interpreted as approval of the conditions of property or its management.

Table 3.3	Advice provided by voluntary organisations on different aspects of housing				
	Housing Advice	Generalist Advice	Specialist Advice	Social Welfare	All
Sample number	17	66	15	44	142
	%	%	%	%	%
Where else to go	82	94	100	98	94
How to register on council list	100	96	80	91	94
How to register on housing association list	100	96	73	93	94
Welfare rights and benefits	88	96	93	93	94
Security of tenure	94	91	93	57	81
Protection from eviction/harassment	100	88	93	59	79
Money, arrears and debt advice	71	92	87	66	79
Availability of supported accommodation	94	61	27	89	70
B&B hotels/hostels	94	64	33	64	65
Resolution of disputes	53	82	47	52	65
Accommodation agencies	94	61	13	61	60
Furnishing schemes	88	52	27	71	59
Rent deposit schemes	77	65	33	48	51
Aids and adaptations	29	61	33	39	47
Vacancies in private sector	82	38	20	50	46

Source: *Telephone survey*

From information to advocacy

3.35   The nature of the advice required may vary as well as its subject matter. Some people may simply require information about the address of an accommodation agency, while others may require intensive and time consuming practical assistance and representation. There are two possible reasons why the need may vary. First, it may reflect objectively different housing problems. A distant threat of eviction may merit, for example, the provision of leaflets on tenants' rights and on homelessness legislation, while a roofless person may require assistance, such as accompanying the client to the homelessness unit and following up the result. Second, people may require levels of assistance commensurate with their personal circumstances. For example, someone whose first language is not English may require more assistance than someone whose English is fluent.

3.36   Typologies of the range of advice services are not hard to find. The simplest advocate a three-part division into "information, advice and aid[10], or the "three As - advice, assistance and advocacy.[11] More elaborate typologies include that of the Advice Services Alliance:

> *Listening* to clients
>
> **diagnosing** the problem
>
> giving **information**
>
> **advising** on the options available
>
> taking **action** on behalf of clients
>
> **negotiating** on their behalf

10. Raynsford, N. (1979) *Housing Aid and Advice in Housing* 15(1), pp.4-8.
11. Casey, L. (1995) 'Together For London's Aid' in *Roof*, May, p.12.

representing clients' cases at tribunals and in courts

referrals where appropriate

alerting policymakers to burning issues affecting us all

informing and **educating** - through talks and publicity materials, for example

developing and **supporting** other organisations

providing **training** on new laws and policies.[12]

3.37   Another list of services is:

straightforward information

explanation

advice such as setting out possible options

practical aid such as helping with form filling

referral to another source of help

mediation

counselling

advocacy.[13]

3.38   This simple classification was adopted in the postal and telephone surveys, and the "secondary" services, such as training and education, and campaigning and policy work which it neglects were examined in the case studies. It provides broadly a spectrum of increasingly complex and resource-intensive services, though it should be noted that mediation and counselling are very different from each other and may not be seen as an intrinsic part of "advice". Mediation, for example, may involve neutrality between protagonists, whereas housing aid work can involve advocating on behalf of clients.

Local authorities

3.39   Five types of advice - straightforward information, explanation, advice (such as setting out possible options), practical aid (such as help with form filling), and referral were provided by most local authorities (Table 3.4). In the case studies it was apparent, though, that the extent of practical aid could vary from one authority to another, and from one day to another depending on pressure of work, particularly in authorities without dedicated advice services. Another four forms were provided by, at most, just over half the local authorities. Of these, mediation was provided most frequently, by just over half the councils, although some officers said it was not provided in all possible cases of disputes. "Counselling" was a problematic term to many respondents, and it is likely that the table overstates its provision, if the term is used to mean provision by trained counsellors. Advocacy for clients in conflict with the council was provided by one third of the local authorities (33%) overall and just over half (52%) of authorities provide advocacy to people not in conflict with the council, but there are substantial differences between different types of authority.

3.40   Generally, councils with dedicated advice services provided the widest range of types of advice. Nine out of ten authorities (91%) with separate advice centres and three quarters (75%) of authorities with separate advice sections provide advocacy for clients not in conflict with the council, whereas only three in ten (28%) of authorities who provided advice only as part of their homeless duties did so. In telephone interviews and in case studies, officers said that a typical example of such advocacy was to challenge the homelessness decisions of colleagues, and some said that they were under instruction or

---

12. Advice Services Alliance (undated) *The Case for Advice 2,000* (leaflet).
13. Scottish Homes (1992) *Housing Information And Advice: You Can't Ask A Leaflet Questions*, Scottish Homes.

informal pressure not to do so. It is hardly surprising then that authorities which do not have advice services outside their homelessness service are less likely to take on this advocacy role. All authorities which restricted their advice role to their statutory duty under the homelessness legislation said they provided straightforward information and referral to other sources of advice, but all other types of advice were less frequently provided than in authorities with other organisational forms of advice service.

Table 3.4	Types of housing advice provided by local authorities (percentages)			
Type of Housing Advice	**Type of Authority**			**All Authorities**
	London Boroughs	Metropolitan Councils	District Councils	
Sample number	22	22	61	105
	%	%	%	%
Straightforward information	100	100	100	100
Referral	100	100	100	100
Explanation	100	100	98	99
Advice	100	100	95	97
Practical Aid	96	100	95	96
Mediation	77	73	41	55
Advocacy: client not in conflict with the council	73	73	38	52
Counselling	46	50	31	38
Advocacy: client in conflict with the council	36	55	25	33

Source: *Telephone survey*

Voluntary organisations

3.41 As with local authorities, virtually all voluntary organisations said they provided straightforward information, explanation, advice, practical aid and referral (Table 3.5). Over three quarters (78%) said they advocated on behalf of clients, almost six in ten (68%) said they provided mediation services, and over four in ten (43%) provided counselling. These proportions were much higher than for district councils. In interviews, voluntary organisation staff seemed clearer than some local authorities about whether or not they provided counselling.

3.42 The perception that statutory sector and generalist advice services tend to concentrate on the information and advice end of the spectrum, and that voluntary sector specialist agencies tend towards the aid and advocacy end is only partly supported by these findings. In fact, generalist voluntary organisations are more likely than local authorities to provide mediation, counselling and advocacy, but the overall results for local authorities obscure the extent to which London boroughs and metropolitan councils do provide these types of advice.

Table 3.5	Types of housing advice provided by voluntary organisations (percentages)				
Form of Housing Advice	Housing Aid	Other Specialist Advice	General Advice	Social Welfare Agencies	All
Sample number	18	14	66	45	143
	%	%	%	%	%
Referral	100	100	100	100	100
Advice	100	100	99	98	99
Straightforward information	100	100	97	100	99
Practical Aid	100	93	100	96	98
Explanation	100	100	96	98	97
Advocacy	83	93	74	76	78
Mediation	44	43	59	67	58
Counselling	39	29	33	65	43

Source: *Postal survey*

Secondary services

3.43 Activities commonly referred to as "secondary" advice work include education, training, development support and consultancy. Some agencies at the national level provided only those sorts of services to "primary" advice agencies. At the local level such secondary agencies also exist. A notable example is the National Homelessness Advice Service which, despite its name, operates at the local level, providing support for the homelessness advice work of CABx and independent advice agencies through the specialist skills of Shelter and a network of consultants. From the case studies it was apparent that some agencies within the local authority and voluntary sectors provide both primary and secondary services. The exact relative provision of secondary services by the two sectors is unknown, but the case studies revealed more provision of secondary services by voluntary organisations than by local authorities.

3.44 The majority of specialist housing advice agencies (57%) said they were front line agencies working directly with the public. But a large minority (43%) said they were back up agencies as well. From the case study evidence this may understate the secondary work such agencies do, for example in providing advice or training to workers in other advice centres. However, some agencies said they would like to do more secondary work if resources permitted.

Summary

3.45 This chapter has reviewed three aspects of housing advice services. First, four *purposes or objectives* of housing advice services were distinguished, termed the citizenship, policy, service rights and market efficiency objectives. In practice these are often carried out simultaneously, although service rights is the most common objective, particularly in the voluntary sector. Market efficiency is not seen as the primary objective of many, despite its popularity with government. Second, some boundaries between housing advice and other housing services, and between housing and other advice services, were delineated, though in practice these are somewhat pragmatically drawn. A wide range of housing problems are the subject of housing advice, and local authorities with dedicated advice services provide advice consistently on more aspects of housing problems than authorities without such services. In the voluntary sector, specialist housing aid centres cover the widest range of subject matter. The chapter concluded with an examination of different types of advice, which showed that most agencies in the voluntary and local authority sectors provide a range of information and basic advice, but that forms of advice such as mediation, advocacy and counselling requiring extensive case-work are provided least by district councils and more by the voluntary sector.

4 Patterns of Provision

4.1   This chapter describes the organisation of housing advice services within local authorities and the pattern of provision by voluntary organisations. The chapter is presented in three parts, starting with an account of the organisation of housing advice services within local government, continuing with a description of the nature of advice provision by voluntary organisations, then finishing with a description of the overall picture of the nature of provision by different types of agency within local authority areas, drawing particularly on case studies.

Two sectors

4.2   Although often motivated from the same concerns about homelessness, poor housing conditions and citizens' rights, local authorities and voluntary organisations have different starting points in their roles as housing advice providers. For a local authority advice provision stems from its statutory powers and duties, and it cannot, within the law, provide an advice service unless there are statutory powers which enable it to - leaving aside resource issues. Although there have been few explicit duties to provide housing advice services, there are a wide range of powers and duties within housing, social services and local government legislation which provide a legal basis for providing fairly comprehensive advice services, often as a means to achieving other service provision. These include provisions in relation to the authority's landlord role, its role in renewal, and in relation to homelessness. As a result, authorities have not generally been inhibited from developing housing advice services.

4.3   Voluntary organisations, in contrast, have freedom to form and to attempt to meet the needs of any group or groups they wish. Many have charitable origins in a concern for the poorly housed or homeless, or in the housing and wider needs of particular disadvantaged groups, such as ethnic minority groups, ex-prisoners, or vulnerable young people. They may develop their role from that of advocate on behalf of particular clients, into campaigner on behalf of the client group. They are not, therefore, required to be neutral in balancing the needs of different client and interest groups, for example, between vulnerable young people and disabled people, or between private tenants and private landlords. In this lies one of their most distinctive differences from local authorities.

4.4   Within one local authority area the pattern of provision that results from voluntary sector involvement might supplement, complement, or overlap with the provision of the local authority. Voluntary organisations may also overlap with each other in their provision, or gaps may exist. No assumptions about the nature of provision can be made, unless it is clear that the local authority and voluntary organisations in an area have a common strategy which clarifies roles. This is unusual.

Types of local authority housing advice service

4.5   As Chapter 2 showed, some local authorities have long had housing advice centres, but the extent of these and other forms of provision was not known. Two thirds of authorities overall (66%) said they operate a housing aid or advice service which has a wider remit than to provide advice to homeless people under Part III of the Housing Act. However, in one in five authorities (19%) this service is provided by staff who also have other duties. So one third of authorities (34%) have no advice service beyond that required by their homelessness duties and fewer than half of authorities overall (46%) have advice services with dedicated staff (Table 4.1).

4.6   Substantial differences were found in the structure of advice provision by different types of authority, with urban (London and metropolitan) authorities far more likely than rural and suburban (district) councils to have more developed services. Almost three quarters of London boroughs (73%) have a dedicated centre, section or staff for housing advice, whereas fewer than one third (31%) of district councils do. Over six in ten (64%) metropolitan councils operate a service with dedicated staff.

4.7   The most common form of dedicated housing advice service is a housing advice section within the housing department, and overall one quarter of authorities (26%) have such a service. One in ten authorities (11%) operates a centre which is separate from the housing department, and a similar proportion (9%) employ staff with a remit only or mainly to provide housing advice, working within a unit or section with other responsibilities (Table 4.1).

Outside the housing department

4.8   Just how independent in organisational terms a dedicated advice service is may depend to some extent on the pattern of accountability within the authority. The majority of housing advice centres and sections are accountable to the Director of Housing. They may fall within the range of responsibilities of a senior officer who is also responsible for the homelessness team, the private sector or housing needs.

Table 4.1	Organisational form of local authority housing advice services (percentages)			
Form of Service	**Type of Authority**			**All Authorities**
	London Boroughs	**Metropolitan Councils**	**District Councils**	
Sample number	23	22	61	106
	%	%	%	%
Separate centre	30	14	3	11
Separate section	39	41	16	26
Separate service	4	9	12	9
Part of staff duties	13	14	23	19
Statutory duties only	13	23	46	34

Source: *Telephone survey*

4.9   The small number of authorities which have chosen to locate housing advice services outside the housing department may have had different reasons for taking this route, but will commonly cite the advantage of independent scrutiny of homelessness decisions as a benefit. This is illustrated in Figure 4.1 which describes the organisation of advice services in Norwich.

Figure 4.1	The organisation of housing advice in Norwich Borough

The Norwich Advice Service (NAS), deals with housing, welfare rights, and consumer advice from within the Law and Administration Department. Staff claim they are able to operate independently of the council's other service departments, with less conflict of interest than in other organisational forms. They suggest that the quality of advice is higher as a result of this comparative freedom. The housing department appreciates having NAS function separately. Staff felt that a housing department advice service would be less well funded, and staff would be less able to develop expertise because of pressures of other work. NAS are able to spur the department and yet are able to maintain closer relations than a voluntary organisation would be able to. In addition NAS are able to act as a training resource.

Investigating applications under homelessness legislation

4.10 Homelessness provides a key focus for advice provision in local authorities but dedicated advice services are not necessarily involved in all aspects of homelessness work. Over half of all local authorities (54%) use a specialist homelessness unit or officer to carry out investigations into applicants under the homelessness legislation. The proportion is higher (71%) in those authorities with specialist housing advice sections within the housing department. This work is carried out by a housing advice service or centre in between 14 and 20 per cent of authorities with dedicated advice services. In authorities with such dedicated services (separate centres, sections or staff) applicants are more usually investigated by homeless units (Table 4.2).

4.11 In some cases the task of investigation was shared. For example, in two case study authorities the advice centre provided the first stage or initial investigation of homelessness applications. Where advice workers assessed that the authorities had no clear duty to provide accommodation (non priority applicants) the advice centres continued to provide case work advice and appropriate assistance to alleviate or avert homelessness. Where it was assessed that the authorities might have a duty to rehouse the applicant, they referred to the homelessness unit for further investigation.

Homelessness advice

4.12 Local authorities have a duty to offer advice and appropriate assistance under Part III of the 1985 Housing Act to people who are found to be homeless but not in priority need, or to be intentionally homeless, in order to enable them to obtain or remain in appropriate accommodation. Authorities are able to interpret the extent of this duty in various ways. Previous research shows that the nature of advice and assistance given varies, and that there has been a growth in the range of advice and assistance provided by local authorities since 1986.[1]

4.13 The Code of Guidance emphasises that authorities should give "active" help, including counselling and referral to other specialist agencies.[2] It suggests that advice on, for example, Housing Benefit and Community Charge Rebates (now Council Tax) may be relevant, as might information on aspects of home purchase, particularly low cost home ownership. It also suggests there may be a need for advice on social issues which have contributed to the applicant's situation such as relationship breakdown, domestic violence, or alcohol and drug abuse.

Table 4.2	Investigations under homelessness legislation: organisation of local authorities (percentages)			
Investigating Body	**Type of Authority**			**All Authorities**
	London Boroughs	Metropolitan Councils	District Councils	
Sample number	23	22	61	106
	%	%	%	%
Housing department - homelessness unit	65	55	49	54
Housing department - other	4	14	28	20
Housing advice service or centre	17	18	5	10
Housing association	0	0	12	7
Other	13	14	7	9

Source: *Telephone survey*

1. Mullins, D. & Niner, P. with Marsh, A. & Walker, B. (1996) *Evaluation of the 1991Homelessness Code of Guidance*, London, HMSO.
2. Department Of The Environment / Department Of Health / Welsh Office (1991) *Homelessness Code Of Guidance For Local Authorities*, (3rd Ed) HMSO.

4.14   Although the code provides some guidance, there remains great scope for authorities to interpret their advice and assistance duty and to organise the service in different ways. The telephone survey and the case studies of housing authorities aimed to find out about the nature of the choices made by authorities.

4.15   One third of authorities (33%) said they provide advice and assistance from an advice service or centre, another one third (35%) provide advice through a specialist homelessness unit or officer, one in ten (9%) uses their decentralised housing offices, and over one in five (23%) provides advice and assistance in other ways, through generic housing department staff, for example. In a small number of cases, all LSVT authorities, it is provided by housing associations, or voluntary organisations (Table 4.3).

4.16   Two thirds of London boroughs (65%) offer this advice through a dedicated housing advice service or centre, while the most common organisational arrangement for district authorities (44%) is to use a specialist homelessness unit or officer to fulfil their duty. Metropolitan authorities mainly use homelessness units or district housing offices. A choice has been made in some authorities, particularly London Boroughs, to separate the administration of the investigation, from the delivery of an advice service which is usually available more widely than to people who have applied for assistance under homelessness legislation. In district councils, the staff who investigate applications under the homelessness legislation also fulfil the authority's obligations in relation to advice and assistance as well as in relation to those who require rehousing. As a consequence, it was not surprising to find in case studies that the scope for officers to play an advocacy role is less in most district councils than in most London boroughs and metropolitan authorities.

Table 4.3	Advice and assistance under homelessness legislation: organisation of local authorities (percentages)			
Advice Provided By	**Type of Authority**			**All Authorities**
	London Boroughs	**Metropolitan Councils**	**District Councils**	
Sample number	23	22	61	106
	%	%	%	%
Advice service or centre	65	18	26	33
Homelessness unit or officer	9	36	44	35
Decentralised housing office	9	23	5	9
Other	17	23	25	23

Source: *Telephone survey*

4.17   The advice and assistance provided by local authorities in discharging their homelessness duty may relate to a number of areas of housing difficulty, and the scope to provide different forms of advice, information and practical assistance is wide. All but one authority offered advice on housing and welfare benefits, on protection from eviction or harassment, and on security of tenure. Over three quarters (77%) said they would help to resolve disputes with friends or relatives with whom the homeless person was living. Four fifths of authorities (82%) agreed that they will liaise with building societies where relevant, and even greater numbers (94%) will liaise with landlords (Table 4.4).

Table 4.4	Housing advice provided by local authorities under homelessness duties (percentages)			
	Type of Authority			All Authorities
	London Boroughs	Metropolitan Councils	District Councils	
Sample number	22	22	61	105
	%	%	%	%
Security of tenure	100	100	100	100
Housing or other welfare benefits	100	100	98	99
Protection from eviction/harassment	100	100	98	99
Information on private renting	95	100	97	97
Information on housing associations and/or co-ops	96	96	97	96
Advice to register on local authority waiting list	100	100	93	96
Liaison with landlords	96	96	93	94
List of B&B hotels or hostels	96	86	84	87
Liaison with building societies	82	82	82	82
Information on accommodation agencies	96	55	87	82
Referral to advice agency	86	73	78	79
Help to resolve disputes with friends of relatives who are accommodating applicants	64	73	84	77
Information on specific private rented sector	68	64	71	69
Referral to rent deposit funds	50	23	64	52
Referral to accommodation register	50	23	54	47
Other advice and help	46	36	43	42

4.18   Most authorities were also able to refer people to other sources of help. Four fifths (79%) referred people to another advice agency, and a similar proportion (82%) offered information on accommodation agencies. Just under half (47%) referred to an accommodation register. Half the authorities surveyed (52%) refer people to rent deposit schemes, and, again, fewer metropolitan authorities (23%) offered this sort of help.

4.19   Information on finding or applying for accommodation is offered frequently. Only those authorities which had transferred their stock to a housing association did not advise non-priority homeless people to apply for a council house. Almost all authorities (96%) offered information on housing associations and co-operatives, and on private renting (97%). Almost seven in ten authorities (69%) were able to offer information on specific vacancies in the private rented sector. Lists of bed and breakfasts, or hostels, were available from almost nine in ten (87%) authorities. Other advice and help was offered by over four in ten (42%) authorities.

Private sector teams   4.20   Dedicated housing advice staff are sometimes located within or close to sections of housing departments which have been established to take a lead role in co-ordinating council services such as environmental health, housing renewal and housing benefit to the private sector. These teams have often been active in developing networks of agencies, such as landlord forums, or mortgage arrears forums throughout the authority area, and these are also relevant to advice services. For example, in Brighton, housing advice and tenancy relations skills are combined in the staff who make up the private sector team. In Birmingham, a central Private Tenancy Unit has created a range of initiatives designed to uphold tenants' rights and protect them, including a helpline for HMO residents, a Private Rented Sector Forum, an accommodation agency, and rent and deposit guarantee schemes.

4.21   Tenancy relations officers (TROs) are employed in most authorities with dedicated advice services (90%), and in more than three quarters of the local authorities surveyed (78%) to assist in the regulation of the private rented sector. They may have wider role than tenant-landlord work. In authorities with dedicated advice centres or sections TROs are likely to be based within the advice service: two thirds (67%) employed in such authorities were based in such sections or centres. In case studies the expertise of TROs was valued by colleagues, and one authority had recently employed an additional TRO. At times TROs have to liaise closely with local authority solicitors as well as housing staff.

Secondary advice services

4.22   As well as offering advice directly to the public, a number of authorities offer other advice related services, such as consultancy and training, commonly referred to as secondary services. These may be available to other staff within the authority, or to the voluntary sector. The purposes include increasing the expertise of a network of advisers, and encouraging referral between agencies. Staff of secondary services said they were able to reach far more clients indirectly, through improving the quality of service offered by advisers who used their services, than if they provided only a direct advice service to clients. One illustration of such a service is the Birmingham Welfare Rights Unit, described in Figure 4.2.

Figure 4.2   Birmingham's Welfare Rights and Money Advice Unit

Birmingham Council operate a Welfare Rights and Money Advice Unit offering advice and consultancy to front line council staff who have direct contact with members of the public. The work is mainly concerned with supporting staff in neighbourhood offices, and social workers. A consultancy line available during working hours is well used. Training provided for council staff by the unit ranges from half day awareness sessions to advanced money and debt advice training. The telephone service is also used by the voluntary sector. The team carries out a small amount of case-work for members of the public (103 people who were facing repossession action in 1995, for example). The unit is also concerned with take up campaigns, and implementing the council's anti-poverty strategy.

Organisational structures in practice

4.23   Some authorities have developed housing advice services separately from their homelessness units deliberately to provide a degree of independence from homelessness decision-making processes. In the case studies, many examples were given of local authority housing advisers providing advice to clients about how to challenge a decision on eligibility under the homelessness laws. Advisers also sometimes assisted tenants of the authority who had not had satisfaction from estate management staff and decentralised offices, even when they had an information and advice role. While advisers and their managers acknowledged that there was a limit to the advocacy role they could play if the client was in dispute with the authority, they also argued that the relative independence they had was useful to clients. Advisers said that they are able to advocate "behind the scenes", in a less confrontational way than other agencies could. They also argue that dedicated advice staff are not overwhelmed by the administration of homelessness duties, and this helps also in the identification of needs which require policy initiatives in response to problems faced by their clients. These points are illustrated in Figures 4.3 and 4.4 which describe the organisation of advice services in Ealing and Colchester Boroughs.

Figure 4.3   The organisation of housing advice in Ealing Borough

The Housing Advice Service (HAS) is part of the Housing Needs Division, along with the Homeless Persons Unit and Sheltered Housing. The Needs Division also administers the housing applications list and allocates vacant properties. HAS is responsible for an initial assessment of a homelessness application, although the decision will rest with the homeless persons unit. If an applicant is found to be ineligible for an offer of accommodation the advice and assistance duty is carried out by the HAS staff.

Figure 4.4   The organisation of housing advice in Colchester Borough

Colchester has had a housing advice centre since 1989 when the housing department was reorganised. Splitting the housing advice and homelessness teams was a convenient decision at the time, not a strategic move, but it has proved to be the right organisational form, officers feel, since neither function is neglected. The homelessness team work in reaction to applications, whereas the advice service is proactive and spends time working with other organisations. There is considerable collaboration on a day-to-day basis between the two teams, and they sometimes undertake joint training.

Housing advice by contract or agreement

4.24   Most authorities provide housing advice services and fulfil their duty to offer advice and assistance under Part III of the Housing Act 1985 by employing staff directly. However a small number of authorities have entered into contracts or agreements with other organisations to provide some advice services. For example, several LSVT authorities have contracted with the housing associations which took over their stock to investigate applications under the homelessness legislation, and to provide advice and assistance as required under homelessness legislation. One district has contracted the work to a housing association which employs one housing adviser, responsible to a senior homelessness officer; and another has contracted all housing management and homelessness services to a housing association, which employs housing advisers responsible to the homelessness and lettings manager. The introduction of a duty to secure more comprehensive housing advice services might require further provision to be ensured.

4.25   Two urban case study authorities had or were making arrangements for the voluntary sector to provide advice services extending beyond homelessness duties while the research was proceeding, and a few other examples of contracts or service level agreements were encountered. Wandsworth was in the process of contracting out a range of advice services to voluntary organisations by negotiation, but would consider competitive tendering in future; and in a much more consensual environment Kirklees was negotiating a service level agreement with CHAS, Kirklees, an independent voluntary sector housing aid centre which the metropolitan council has funded on a relatively large scale over many years. Kirklees does not employ dedicated housing advice staff to provide advice and assistance beyond their homelessness duty.

Voluntary sector patterns of provision

4.26   A rich diversity of voluntary organisations of all types exist in all parts of Britain, and, in the advice field, the Citizens' Advice Bureaux movement has extended into every large town and city throughout England. However, there is also evidence that voluntary organisations thrive in urban areas where local authorities have had a positive attitude to funding them, particularly as a way of demonstrating a commitment to the most vulnerable or disadvantaged groups in an area.[3] In the local authority sector, advice services in rural areas are less well developed than in urban areas, and this study sought to establish whether this was the case for the voluntary sector as well.

3.   Stoker, G. (1991) *The Politics of Local Government*, London: Macmillan, pp. 132-135.

4.27   Voluntary organisations see three advantages in their involvement in advice work: flexibility, independence and responsiveness. These advantages are recognised by many local authorities, although authorities also claim independence, responsiveness and flexibility. It is generally accepted, for example, that local government officers cannot represent or advocate for clients in some circumstances.

4.28   It is understandable that both sectors seek to establish their value, and whatever the truth of specific claims, there was a large degree of agreement that both sectors have a role in housing advice provision. The following sections are concerned with mapping the nature of that role within the voluntary sector.

Numbers and types of voluntary organisations
Housing aid services

4.29   Most housing aid centres in the voluntary sector are affiliated to Shelter or CHAS. There are also a small number of independent HACs, which are often affiliated to FIAC. Shelter has the largest network: there are 37 Shelter Housing Aid Centres and projects in England of which 23 are managed directly and 14 are independent centres funded by Shelter. They are largely concentrated in the South East region, with limited cover in the North of England.

4.30   The HACs provide both direct and support services:

"Shelter has several models of direct service delivery: frontline, 'second tier' and special projects. Frontline HACs provide services directly to members of the public and to other organisations. 'Second Tier' centres only provide housing aid to workers in advice centres. Our special projects ... provide specialist advice to specific groups."[4]

4.31   The second largest network is that of the Catholic Housing Aid Society (CHAS), which serves any client, irrespective of religion, gender, ethnicity, or sexual orientation. It contains 11 groups including central London which co-ordinates the others, as well as acting as a housing aid centre itself. All are independently constituted. The largest is CHAS Kirklees, which has two offices, in Huddersfield and Dewsbury, as well as providing outreach services.

Specialist centres

4.32   There are 48 independent law centres in England, mainly based in large metropolitan areas. Other specialist advice services concentrate on money and debt advice, or welfare rights and benefits. It is not known how many such agencies exist throughout England, but there has been a growth in recent years as poverty has intensified amongst more vulnerable groups such as lone parents and unemployed people, and as debt has become established as a frequent cause of homelessness.

Home improvement agencies

4.33   Home improvement agencies (HIAs) have developed in the voluntary sector to serve the growing number of older people in owner occupation. From 1978 Shelter and Anchor Housing Trust established Care and Repair and Staying Put projects respectively. HIAs assist older people to cope with repairs and maintenance, and with any adaptations that may assist them to remain in their home. The issues on which advice is required may include welfare benefits, improvement grants, technical guidance, evaluating builders' estimates, and obtaining loan finance. The type of advice may vary from information to advocacy.

4.34   The Department of the Environment has provided funding for HIAs since 1986, and since 1991 monies have been channelled through local authorities. The Department and local authority housing and social services budgets are the main sources of funds, and charitable donations are also sought.

---

4.   Shelter (1995) *Housing Services Division Information Pack*, section 3.

Generalist agencies

4.35 So-called general advice provision is dominated by the CAB movement. CABx have the widest coverage of any advice organisation in the voluntary sector. There are around 725 bureaux in England, with more than double this number of outlets for advice, through surgeries and outreach sessions to improve access. They are organised as a federation at national level in the National Association of Citizens Advice Bureaux, which also has eight regional offices with a development role. The survey and case studies of local authorities showed that only one local authority area did not have a CAB available to people living in its area. Thirty eight per cent had one CAB outlet, and nine per cent had five or more.

4.36 Other general advice agencies operate at neighbourhood or city or other local levels, and may be members of the Federation of Independent Advice Centres (FIAC). Their character varies greatly, encompassing volunteer-run, part-time agencies operating from a community centre, to large, funded projects with staff and premises of their own and providing a range of specialist as well as "generalist" services to anyone who asks.

Social welfare agencies

4.37 The variety of social welfare agencies was discussed in the last chapter. Broadly they may play two roles: as referral agencies and as direct advice providers. For example, groups formed by people from ethnic minorities for social and cultural reasons may play a valuable role in referring members to advice agencies, and local residents groups are also known to play this role. In contrast, voluntary agencies, such as those which run day shelters and night shelters, may work intensively with vulnerable groups such as young homeless people and may provide a more holistic advocacy and support service than the most specialist housing aid centre can do. Such organisations are key players in the provision of housing advice to single people who are homeless or threatened with homelessness. The nature of the housing advice role of these agencies and its effectiveness is little researched.

Housing advice roles

4.38 The sample for the postal survey shows the variety and mix of voluntary organisations. Six types of organisation were surveyed: housing aid centres, mainly those in the Shelter and CHAS networks; general advice centres, mainly CABx; specialist advice centres such as law centres and welfare rights services; groups which serve particular client groups, such as older people, vulnerable young people or disabled people; and organisations which work with and on behalf of homeless people. An average of 7.2 organisations for each area were surveyed. The number varied from one in a small, rural district to 37 in a large city.

4.39 The extent of an agency's role in housing advice may vary from being its sole or main role, as in a Shelter housing aid centre, to being part of a wider welfare role, as in a service targeted on young people. How the voluntary organisations in our sample described their housing advice role is shown in Table 4.5.

Table 4.5	Voluntary organisations' housing advice role (percentages)			
Housing Advice Role	**London Boroughs**	**Metropolitan Councils**	**District Councils**	**All Authorities**
Sample number	40	54	54	148
	%	%	%	%
Sole or main role	10	11	11	11
Part of wider advice role	70	43	61	57
Part of wider welfare role	15	28	13	19
Part of role as housing provider	5	19	15	14

Source: *Postal survey*

Area of operation

4.40 Although the sample was based on local authority areas, no assumption could be made about the geographical area of operation of the voluntary organisations. When asked what area they served, the more specialist services said they cover a wider geographical area than generalist advice services. Over half (54%) overall, however, defined themselves as covering the whole of a local authority district area, and 13 per cent cover a county rather than a district or borough. Only three per cent of the organisations described themselves as serving a neighbourhood or estate, although in case studies it was suggested that, while an organisation serves a wide area, the majority of clients may live or work nearby. Residents' organisations were excluded from the sample, so their role as advice providers and referral agencies is unreported here.

Primary and secondary services

4.41 The distinction between "primary" advice services, which provide advice directly to clients in need, and "secondary" services, which support the work of primary services with training, information, development and consultancy services, has been made already. In case studies, the majority of agencies were found to provide both primary and secondary services. For example, a CAB may be primarily concerned with providing an advice service to the public, but may also train staff from other voluntary organisations in issues such as money advice. A Shelter HAC may be primarily concerned with providing secondary services of training and consultancy, but will often take on the more difficult housing advice casework.

Patterns of provision in practice

4.42 Given the diversity in the nature of provision in the voluntary and local authority sectors, it is clear that the pattern of provision is likely to vary from one locality to another. At one extreme end of a spectrum, the local authority might see its role as restricted to the provision of advice and assistance to applicants under the homelessness laws, and there may be one CAB in the largest town which handles a proportion of housing enquiries but has no access to specialist expertise and is not within the area covered by the National Homelessness Advisory Service. Such areas are likely to be relatively rural and sparsely populated, and may also have relatively low levels of need, but whatever need exists seems less well provided for than in many more urban areas. This overall picture needs qualification by reference to the relative lack of advice services in some urban areas and the initiatives taken in some rural areas to expand advice provision, for example through a telephone advice line in Lincolnshire.

4.43 Large and medium authority areas might have a larger range of advice services. Figures 4.5, 4.6 and 4.7 describe the pattern of provision in Kirklees, Brighton, and Birmingham, which provide contrasting examples of areas with well-developed networks of housing advice providers and a distinctive approach.

Conclusion

4.44 A variety of forms and patterns of housing advice provision were identified through the research and this chapter focused on what emerged as the key forms of housing advice, and the related organisational arrangements in addressing homelessness and wider housing advice needs. The findings confirm the expected diversity in the patterns of provision between different types of area, and within them. Almost half the local authorities showed commitment to the provision of advice within their organisational and staffing structure; and, in the voluntary sector, provision extends beyond specialist housing aid centres - which do not operate everywhere - to other types of advice agencies, and to organisations better known for their social welfare role in which advice is one amongst several functions.

Figure 4.5   Housing advice in Kirklees

Kirklees is a metropolitan area with a population of over 375,000 in West Yorkshire. CHAS Kirklees receives a grant from the council on the understanding that it provides as comprehensive an advice service as possible to complement the council's role. The council has no identifiable housing advice centre, although homelessness officers provide advice and assistance as well as referring clients to CHAS. The council also employs two tenancy relations officers, and many other staff, such as private sector housing and estate management staff, play a role in advice work. CHAS employs 17 staff, based in two offices in Huddersfield and Dewsbury. There is also outreach work, and a shop has been opened in partnership with other agencies in Heckmondwike, one of the least accessible small towns in Kirklees. Other advice agencies include the council's own Benefit Advice Service and a network of four Service Information Points managed by social services staff. In the voluntary sector, there are four CABx, several groups serving the needs of ethnic minority groups, one Staying Put project, one women's refuge, one students' union welfare centre and one accommodation agency. Several housing associations provide temporary or follow-on accommodation for vulnerable groups, and several other agencies provide services for other disadvantaged groups. A newly-established law centre refers housing enquiries to CHAS, by agreement. There are several demonstrations of close working relationships, such as the presence of staff or committee members from one organisation on the committee of another, and in services such as a court-based advice desk, provided jointly by a number of agencies on a rota basis. Senior staff from CHAS meet senior council staff in a number of forums.

Figure 4.6   Housing advice in Brighton

Brighton, a seaside town on the south coast, has a population of over 140,000. The council's housing advice centre provides advice and assistance to callers and acts as the reception point for its housing department, which contains a team of housing advisers/tenancy relations officers. There is a homelessness unit which refers to housing advisers for advice and assistance anyone who does not qualify for accommodation. Other council services include a Welfare Rights Advice Service which stresses its proactive, secondary role, as well as its casework. The largest voluntary sector provider is the Brighton Housing Trust's Housing Aid and Legal Centre, which was a housing aid centre until it recently took on a legal role, under contract to the council, after a law centre closed. It is a member of the Shelter network, and acts as a base for the NHAS. The housing advice work includes an accommodation agency and is funded from a variety of sources, including central and local government grants. The Brighton Housing Trust provides a range of services for vulnerable and homeless people, including a day centre and a supported accommodation project for single people who have been homeless. Other voluntary sector agencies include the CAB, an unemployed workers centre, and a money advice centre. Close working relationships between many of the agencies can be seen, for example on the Private Sector Housing Forum, which is serviced by the council, and has a steering group chaired by the director of the Brighton Housing Trust.

Figure 4.7   Housing advice in Birmingham

Birmingham's 43 Neighbourhood Offices are designed to operate as an access point to all council services, and more broadly to advice people on local services and facilities. One advice worker estimated that a quarter of the 1,000,000 enquiries dealt with each year are related to housing, and a further quarter are on money issues including housing benefit and mortgage/rent arrears. Clients may have their query answered by the receptionist, but those with more complex queries are offered an appointment with a generic adviser, who it is said will consider all aspects of a problem. Local knowledge, and being outside the departmental structure, are regarded as advantages in this approach. In addition housing advice and secondary support services are offered by the Private Tenancy Unit (PTU) which has a city wide brief. The PTU is co-ordinating a number of initiatives designed to improve the amount and quality of housing available for private renting and to encourage best practice among landlords, including a private rented sector forum, and an 'Owners Charter' registering private rented sector properties.

There are a large number of voluntary sector organisations offering housing advice throughout the city. All the major national housing advice agencies are represented, as well as many local groups. The majority of city council funding to housing related voluntary services is concerned with agencies providing hostel accommodation, and other than through the Neighbourhood Offices, funding for housing advice is not prioritised. The council recognises the importance of choice for people seeking advice, but considers it important that it continues to take the lead role in advice provision. There are a number of forums focusing on housing and homelessness, and there is a growing recognition of a need for improved networks as a means of improving service delivery. A recent initiative is the establishment of a forum on housing advice, bringing together voluntary sector agencies.

5 Clients

5.1   This chapter discusses the clients of housing advice services and seeks to answer questions about who they are, whether services reach the clients they aim to reach, how services are provided, and how accessible services are. It draws on the results of interviews, the telephone and postal surveys, the case studies, and interviews with national agencies. The scope of this study did not include systematic interviewing of clients of housing advice services, but wherever possible the researchers listened to the experience of clients in the course of the case studies, and collected information about client evaluations of advice services carried out by case study local authorities and voluntary organisations.

Who needs housing advice?
Estimating need

5.2   The question "Who needs housing advice?" can, in theory, be answered with reference to individual felt need, about which little is known systematically; or with reference to standards, for example set down in legislation, or by professional judgement. In practice, needs for housing advice are identified by professionals and policy makers, drawing on their assessment of demand for existing services and on contact with people in housing difficulty. They may also take into account developments in social policy, and knowledge of demographic and economic trends.

5.3   Three factors were said by local authorities and voluntary organisations to influence them in considering who may need housing advice:

● *the changing role of local government*

   The diversification of social rented and greater reliance on private rented housing to meet housing needs means some consumers need assistance in gaining access to the rented sector, and with any problems that may arise.

● *care in the community policy*

   The needs of particular groups and the development of care in the community are seen to require special efforts to ensure appropriate advice and referral. Where individual clients have more complex housing needs and are vulnerable because of their circumstances or problems, then a more intensive case work approach involving a number of agencies is seen as essential. The implications of this will be considered further in the next chapter.

● *housing market change*

   The growth of owner occupation, and the incidence of housing debt in recent years, has led to some new services, and general concern about the adequacy of advice provision for this group.

5.4   Services are often developed to meet particular needs perceived by service providers, clients make use of them, and so agencies conclude there is a need. It is, however, possible that needs are not being met, or services are not reaching potential clients because of the way they are delivered. No evidence of such a mismatch between needs and services was detected, though many agencies were not satisfied that they had overcome the problem of making their services sufficiently accessible to those they consider to be most in need.

Clients

5.5   In general, statutory and voluntary agencies say their clients are poor and disadvantaged as actors in the private housing market. They are often single people or single parents, and they are homeless or potentially homeless, or living in insecure, bad or inappropriate housing circumstances. A significant number of clients are vulnerable as a result of youth, old age, or health problems, or due to other problems arising from relationships with partners, family members, or landlords. Housing problems are regularly associated with debts and other financial problems which make for difficulties in meeting housing costs. Such disadvantage exacerbates problems common to housing careers (setting up home independently), and to personal crises (such as relationship breakdown) which so often precipitate the search for the advice needed to resolve the housing problems.[1]

5.6   The most pressing need of all is homelessness. Case study local authorities and voluntary organisations said that they have responded to increasing homelessness amongst single people, young people under 25 years, black and ethnic minority groups, refugees and owner occupiers. Front-line homelessness services are particularly targeted to prevent younger homeless people (16 and 17 years old) from sleeping on the streets.

5.7   In addition housing advisers and homelessness agencies reported that they are having to develop new skills and approaches to respond better to the complex needs of some vulnerable groups with multiple needs, including mental health problems, and drugs or alcohol dependency. Finally, the experience of local authorities and voluntary agencies stresses that peoples' needs change over time.

Who is targeted?
Local authorities

5.8   Local authorities with housing advice services which extend beyond their homelessness advice and assistance duty were asked to whom the service or centre was available. Nine out of ten (91%) make their service available to all, including two in ten (20%) who also target specific groups. The remaining one in ten (9%) targets specific groups (Table 5.1). Many emphasised that they would provide some help or refer elsewhere enquirers who do not fall into their target groups. Inner London boroughs stand out as being far more likely to target than other types of authority, with almost two thirds (63%) targeting services, including one quarter (25%) who are also available to all. This was more than twice as many authorities as the overall picture for England, in which fewer than three in ten (29%) targeted services, including one in five (20%) who were available to all.

Table 5.1	Availability of local authority housing advice services (percentages)				
Availability			**Type of Authority**		**All Authorities**
	London Boroughs		**Metropolitan Councils**	**District Councils**	
	Inner	**Outer**			
Sample number	8	12	16	35	71
	%	%	%	%	%
Available to all	38	50	75	86	72
Available to all, but targeted on specific groups	25	42	19	11	20
Targeted on specific groups	38	8	6	3	9

Source: *Telephone survey*

5.9   For those (29% or 20 authorities) who targeted their advice service, the target groups were usually defined with reference to tenure or age group of the client. The most frequently quoted target groups were private tenants (20 mentions), and people who

---

1. Shelter (1995) *Cress Monitoring Statistics 1994/5.*

were homeless or threatened with homelessness (18 mentions). This result confirms the impression received in case study visits when problems of access, disrepair, harassment, and insecurity were said to constitute a large proportion of the work of some advice services. Other target groups mentioned were young people (13 mentions), single people (14 mentions), and owner occupiers (13 mentions), whose needs have been perceived as growing since 1990. Less frequently mentioned were older people, disabled people, ethnic minority groups and housing association tenants.

Voluntary organisations

5.10   The voluntary organisations surveyed were less likely than local authorities to offer their housing advice service to all, although overall three quarters (74%) did, including almost two in ten (18%) who also target specific groups. One in five (20%) targets specific groups (Table 5.2). There were differences between different types of agency, as would be expected, with CABx, for example, confirming their availability to all, and some other voluntary groups focusing on particular needs. Specialist housing aid services were found to be either available to all, or available to all but targeted at certain groups, whereas almost three in ten (29%) of other types of specialist advice services were only available to specific groups.

Table 5.2	Availability of housing advice services provided by voluntary organisations (percentages)				
	Housing Aid	Other Specialist Advice	General Advice	Social Welfare Agencies	All
Sample number	17	14	63	44	138
	%	%	%	%	%
Available to all	47	50	87	16	56
Available to all but targeted on specific groups	53	7	3	30	18
Targeted	0	29	10	41	20
Other	0	14	0	14	6

Source: *Postal survey*

5.11   The most frequently mentioned target group was homeless people. Not surprisingly, all voluntary organisations established to serve homeless people saw them as a target group, and so did all housing associations who targeted their services, and over six in ten general advice services who targeted. Young people were next most frequently targeted, followed by single people. It is less common for voluntary agencies than local authorities to target people living in a particular tenure, although over three in ten target private tenants (34%).

Who is reached?

5.12   Local authorities and voluntary organisations were asked how many enquiries and enquirers were handled by their housing advice service in the year 1994/95. For local authorities it soon became evident that the answers - from 215 to 30,000 enquiries, and from 215 to 77,488 enquirers - were meaningless unless assurances could be obtained that the authorities were collecting information on the same basis. In the case studies it was evident that this was not the case.

5.13   Many authorities surveyed could not provide any figures at all, sometimes because they were reluctant to release information which could be misinterpreted, and sometimes because the only systematic information collected related to enquiries arising from their statutory homelessness duties. While some could provide a figure for the number of enquiries, fewer could provide a figure for the number of enquirers.

5.14   The figures from voluntary organisations similarly need to be treated with caution. It is not possible to compare the figures given between types of agency, and sometimes between individual agencies. The answers ranged from 40 new enquiries of which seven were on housing matters, to 41,448 new enquiries. Fewer than half the agencies surveyed could give us information on numbers of total new enquiries or new enquiries relating to housing. As with local authorities, more voluntary organisations recorded the total number of enquiries than recorded how many enquirers with housing problems they had seen in 1994/95.

5.15   Authorities have developed their own systems for recording the number of enquiries handled. Over seven in ten authorities (73%) said they recorded the characteristics of clients in a standardised way, as do almost two thirds of voluntary organisations (66%). In local authorities there is little if any standardisation in practice. Some authorities did not record telephone enquiries; some recorded second and subsequent visits by clients as separate cases; some authorities recorded enquiries only if they became "cases" involving significant case-work from an adviser, and some recorded them, whatever the level of advice given. There was no method for recording enquiries which was generally accepted by authorities as satisfactory, although some of the details of clients was collected on a similar or common basis. In the voluntary sector, there was more standardisation in the collection of data, due to the influence or requirements of NACAB, FIAC, Shelter and CHAS. The use made of this data is discussed in Chapter 8.

5.16   Broadly two different approaches to collecting information about clients can be detected in local authorities. In the authorities with no identifiable advice service, and in some of the other authorities, information was collected about clients only in order to administer the homelessness provisions of the Housing Act 1985. In some cases the forms used provide no pre-coding, suggesting that very limited use of the information is made for monitoring purposes. In other cases, particularly where housing advice centres and sections exist, fuller information is collected, and usually partly pre-coded so that a profile of service users can be built up.

5.17   Generally, authorities with dedicated advice staff were most likely to collect systematic information, and the general impression of poor monitoring needs to be qualified by the knowledge that some authorities have fairly sophisticated recording systems, particularly those with advice centres separate from the housing department, or dedicated advice sections within the housing department, as Chapter 8 shows.

Client groups
Applicants who are homeless or threatened with homelessness

5.18   As homelessness applications grew in the 1980s local authority and voluntary sector housing advice services were increasingly concerned to prevent as well as alleviate homelessness. Innovations in advice provision, such as telephone services, and in easing access to accommodation, such as rent deposit schemes, often grew out of the perception of growing problems, particularly for some client groups, including single people.

5.19   Case studies demonstrated wide variation in policies and practices towards single homeless people. For example, some local authorities have developed special advice and support initiatives for single homeless people and for young people in particular, including youth housing support services and supported accommodation. Others have developed specialist services in partnership with voluntary agencies. In interviews housing and homelessness officers regularly identified the need for specialist services in order to improve the accessibility, quality and flexibility of advice services.

5.20   For non-priority applicants in general, previous studies as well as this one have shown how local authorities offer advice and assistance,[2] including how to register on

---

2.   Niner, P. (1989) *Homelessness In Nine Local Authorities: Case Studies Of Policy and Practice*, Department Of The Environment/ HMSO; Mullins, D. & Niner, P. with Marsh, A. & Walker, B. (1996) *Evaluation of the 1991 Homelessness Code of Guidance*, London, HMSO.

waiting lists,[3] providing lists of accommodation options and a range of other advice.[4] Homelessness staff in previous studies as well as this one stressed that the quality of advice on offer varies according to day to day service pressures and demands and some homelessness officers reported that some days can be dominated almost entirely by three or four particularly complex cases. Housing advice staff, in contrast, can manage their time more easily to ensure all clients are given a reasonable amount of time for interviews and following case work.

5.21   The case studies showed that, in addition to the advice provided by local authority homelessness and housing advice services, advice may be given to homeless people, or to those threatened with homelessness, by a number of different parts of the local authority and by voluntary organisations. For example, applicants who are threatened with homelessness because of the conditions of repair or management in privately rented accommodation may be able to gain assistance from a council tenancy relations officer; owner occupiers in difficulty with paying their mortgage may be able to receive advice from a welfare benefits team in a social services or chief executive's department, or from a voluntary sector money advice centre part-funded by the council. It is crucial that clients are directed to the most appropriate source of advice, an issue examined in Chapter 6.

Women, children and relationship breakdown

5.22   Women with children were identified as a key group by many housing advice agencies. One of the most significant causes of homelessness and threatened homelessness is relationship breakdown and this pattern applies to all age groups, with significant implications for housing advice services. Women escaping from abusive situations were particularly recognised as being in need of access to advice. A very high proportion of hostel residents are single men who have experienced relationship breakdown.

5.23   Relationship breakdown regularly results in movements between tenures, particularly from owner occupation and private renting into the local authority sector.[5] This gives local authorities a dual role, as adviser and landlord. Tenants undergoing relationship breakdown may require advice on matters such as arrears, respective obligations of the parties to a tenancy agreement, legal rights to transfer property, and tenancy rights in the case of co-habitation; or about the options for rehousing for one of the parties. Local authorities, along with solicitors, play a very major role in providing advice and assistance.

5.24   The indications are that policies and practices vary significantly in this area: "Although the majority of authorities routinely granted joint tenancies to couples, very few made a point of giving advice and information, either in tenants' handbooks or face-to-face, about the implications of shared rights and responsibilities to the tenancy should relationship breakdown occur.[6]

5.25   Many women, with or without children, stay "care of" family and friends prior to seeking help from agencies; and large-scale or significantly male hostel accommodation will not be suitable for women with children. The unsuitability of direct access accommodation has encouraged the development of specialist advice, support and accommodation services for women.

3.   Institute Of Housing (1988) *Who Will House the Homeless?*, Institute Of Housing.
4.   Evans, A. & Duncan, S. (1988) *Responding To Homelessness: Local Authority Policy And Practice*, Department of the Environment / HMSO: Mullins, D. & Niner, P. with Marsh, A. & Walker, B. (1996) *Evaluation of the 1991 Homelessness Code of Guidance*, London, HMSO.
5.   Holmans, A. (1989) 'Divorce and Housing Demand and Need' in Symon, P. *Housing and Divorce*, Centre for Housing Research, University of Glasgow.
6.   Bull, J. (1995) *The Housing Consequences of Relationship Breakdown*, Discussion Paper 10, Centre for Housing Policy, University of York p.17.

Private tenants

5.26 Two major groups of clients in most housing advice services are people seeking a private sector tenancy, or private sector tenants who seek information and advice about their rights. Tenancy relations officers (TROs) and Housing Benefit officers can play a key role. In the case of tenancy relations services, advice and information often shade in to advocacy and implementation of their legal role in enforcement. One case study TRO worked with the police service to raise awareness about illegal eviction of tenants. A booklet setting out the legal position and suggesting how such situations should be handled was produced and distributed to police officers by the police service.

Owner occupiers in debt

5.27 Housing advisers in the voluntary and statutory sectors have perceived an increased need for information and advice services for existing and prospective owner occupiers especially since 1990, as the recession in employment and property prices had an impact on the sustainablity of owner occupation, especially for people on low incomes.

5.28 Over one million households are expected to move house or to purchase for the first time in a year and there is a growing recognition amongst the mortgage lenders and bodies such as the Council for Mortgage Lenders that information and advice are essential if clients are to make sound choices. The Household Mortgage Corporation, for example, identifies three key stages in the homebuyers career - the first time buy, young couples seeking to trade up, and the family needing a larger home. Different issues prevail at these different stages and a decision map has been developed to inform the purchaser about the options, and implications of negative equity, prior to seeking independent mortgage advice.[7]

5.29 Owner occupiers in difficulty may turn for help to a range of agencies in the first instance and advisers reported that an early warning system is essential. Debt problems may first emerge through individuals' contacts with building societies, courts, solicitors, housing associations and advice agencies, such as housing aid centres and CAB. Others may turn for help to local authorities, including homelessness services. Others do not seek help at all, until they reach a crisis such as threatened repossession. Local authority and voluntary sector agencies have set up services intended to reach people who get to this point without seeking advice. For example, advice agencies in Huddersfield have collaborated with the court in running an advice desk in the county court on days when repossession orders are considered. In many areas agencies have extended debt counselling services, in one case study CAB, for example, by using legal aid funding to employ a full-time debt counsellor. Another example is described in Figure 5.1. Advisers emphasise that debt counselling is time-consuming and usually involves debts apart from housing. Advocacy with creditors and searching for alternative housing and other options means that case loads have to be restricted to ensure that follow-up work can be done. It was stated in interviews that whilst debt counselling services have increased in number, clients increasingly have larger levels of multiple debt, making repayment negotiations more difficult.

Figure 5.1   Newcastle CAB Debt Service

The CAB's debt service was initially funded by a charitable Trust, however it is now funded jointly by the local authority and by building societies, both of which have increasingly recognised the significance of debt advice. There are four full-time debt case workers, one of whom is the case worker at the County Court, where a drop-in session is held from 10 to 12 a.m. Volunteers may also be trained to assist with debt work. A typical client may have two priority debts and over five creditors; they may have mortgage and council tax as well as credit card debts. Whilst it is often feasible to negotiate arrangements on loans and credit cards, sometimes a local bank just will not wait.

---

7. Household Mortgage Corporation (1995) *HMC Offers Easy to Follow Help for Bewildered Homebuyers*, Household Mortgage Corporation Circular 3.07.1995.

5.30   Voluntary agencies involved in debt counselling value the contribution of secondary services and one recent evaluation stresses that the most effective and accessible support services are locally or regionally based.[8] CABx and independent advice centres providing debt advice receive support from the NACAB and FIAC respectively. FIAC's debt support service provides specialist advice and information, concentrating on encouraging small, local services to respond to debt problems with a more proactive, better-informed and systematic approach.

5.31   Finally there has been a growth in targeted advice services provided with funding from the private sector. Recent initiatives include a Consumer Credit Counselling Service in Leeds, and Birmingham Debt Line and Money Advice Support Units. Their aim is to improve the quality of money advice services, partly through consultancy and training services for CABx money advice work. These supplement the work of NACAB in relation to CABx.

Older people

5.32   Older people have been a particular focus in housing and social policy for many years and the development of community care policy has emphasised the value of enabling older people to remain in their own homes if appropriate and practical. The advice and assistance they may require to do so, or to achieve a move to a more suitable home, is one focus of attention for many of the agencies surveyed, and not just Care and Repair and Staying Put projects (see 4.33 - 4.34). Another focus is the advice required by older residents of hostels and hospitals, who may have spent many years in an institutional setting, and who may have a disability.

5.33   Agencies emphasised that providing advice and assistance to older people, particularly those with medical or other needs, it is essential to achieve collaboration between health, social services, housing and other agencies. Voluntary organisations, including local Age Concern groups, often play a key role in identifying older people in need of specialist advice, and so need to be aware of the network of advice agencies and services available. Some case study local authorities identified the growth in the proportion of older people in the population as an issue for the future, and a few agencies in both sectors were particularly concerned that housing advice services may not be reaching older members of ethnic minority groups.

Black and ethnic minority groups

5.34   The housing advice needs of black and ethnic minority groups were recognised particularly by councils and voluntary organisations in inner London. One study of housing advice services in London reports that of single people seeking housing advice in June 1992, 55 per cent were of UK European origin; ten per cent were African; seven per cent were Caribbean; nine per cent were Irish; eight per cent were non-UK European; three per cent were from the Indian subcontinent and nine per cent were noted as other.[9] Since then many agencies have been concerned with refugee issues related to new policy and legal developments, such as the Habitual Residence Test and the law on Asylum.[10]

5.35   In some districts it appeared that there was no specific targeting of housing advice services at black or ethnic minority needs. In others, housing agencies seek to assist communication with the use of interpretation services and translation of leaflets and other information. In some local authority districts, (for example, Newcastle) the local authority has developed a proactive approach (including outreach services). In others (for example, Liverpool), specific voluntary organisations have targeted services at the needs of young black people.

8.   Bull, G. (1995) 'Debt in the 90s', *Advisor* (52), pp.35-37.
9.   SHAC (1994) *Advice Services for Single Homeless People in London*, SHAC / Joseph Rowntree.
10. Quilgar, D. (1993) *Housing Provision for Refugees*, Centre for Housing Policy, University of York.

5.36   Some of the agencies emphasised the need to review the effectiveness and targeting of services. They reported their concern that some ethnic minority groups were not using traditional housing advice services and that voluntary organisations representing ethnic minorities were not always part of housing advice networks. As black and ethnic minority groups tend to be concentrated in certain neighbourhoods, in a few districts strategies have been developed in partnership with ethnic minority organisations, to improve the targeting of information and advice services. A further aspect of targeting is the development of services for particular needs, for example, services for young black women. It was suggested that this is essential to modify the effects of male-dominated services.

People with mental health problems

5.37   Community care policies since 1990 and the contraction of long-stay hospitals was paralleled by a growing awareness of the advice and support needs of people with mental health problems who are living in ordinary housing or on the street, including some young people. Concerns were raised, during the case study interviews with local authority and voluntary agencies, about individuals with mental health problems who had been discharged from hospital services and at some point subsequently presented to homelessness agencies. This group was considered to be particularly vulnerable to being caught in the "revolving door" between homelessness, hospitalisation and offending.[11]

5.38   Local authority housing departments are increasingly required to work with social and health services in community care planning and assessments - for example, in relation to tenants with mental health problems with arrears, in relation to neighbour problems, or in the case of hospitalisation or hospital discharge. All these issues have housing advice and wider support implications for officers or hostel staff.

People with physical disabilities

5.39   Mainstream housing providers are now recognising the pleas of Disability Groups for better quality and better co-ordinated information and advice services.[12] For example, two districts illustrate better co-ordinated information about the housing needs of people with a physical disability, and about the stock of accommodation which has been developed, adapted or is adaptable to meet peoples' needs within the district. In Derby a housing association, Walbrook Housing Association, runs a service emphasising that seven needs must be satisfied to make independent and integrated living a realistic proposition - information, counselling, housing, technical aids and equipment, personal assistance, transport and access.[13] In Liverpool a service was developed by a housing association, but subsequently transferred to and managed by the local authority, Liverpool City Council.

People with learning disabilities

5.40   People with learning disabilities also present for help or come to the attention of housing advice or homelessness agencies. The thrust of community care has meant that increasing numbers of people with learning disabilities remain in ordinary housing, whether alone or with their families. This has obvious implications as parents or carers age or die. There has also been an increasing rate of discharge of people with learning disabilities from hospital care into the community as a result of institutional closures and contractions. In parallel, there has been a notable growth in supported accommodation within most districts, provided by local authorities and housing associations, often in partnership with voluntary organisations.

5.41   Homelessness and housing staff commented that, as in the field of mental health, front-line staff required familiarisation about learning disabilities and related housing issues. Learning disabilities is a term applied to a very wide range of abilities and a person with a learning disability may also have a physical disability, or a mental health problem;

---

11. Fisher, K. & Collins, J. (1993) *Homelessness, Health Care, and Welfare Provision*, Routledge.
12. Morris, J. (1993) *Independent Lives, Community Care, and Disabled People*, Macmillan Press.
13. Walbrook Housing Association (1992) *Cracking Housing Problems: Setting up and Running a Specialist Housing Service for Disabled People*, First edition July 1992.

some may also be pregnant or have children. Moreover, concerns were highlighted that people with learning disabilities may be particularly vulnerable to exploitation or pressures, whether they are tenants or homeless people. Addressing the information and advice needs of people with learning disabilities therefore requires patience and time, sensitivity to these issues, and links with appropriate housing and support providers (including social and health services and voluntary organisations).

Vulnerable and homeless young people

5.42   Over the past decade urban and rural districts experienced a growth in youth homelessness, and social housing agencies have accommodated a growing proportion of tenants under 25 years. Larger housing departments which had allocated flats to homeless young people or to young housing applicants regularly found that they experienced difficulties in sustaining tenancies. Against this background certain departments developed specialist youth housing support services (for example, Newcastle's First Move scheme), independently or working in partnership with social services and voluntary agencies.

5.43   A division of labour appears to operate in relation to housing departments and voluntary organisations, whereby the housing departments and some voluntary agencies provide assessment, advice and support aiming to achieve viable and lasting tenancies, whilst social services or other voluntary agencies concentrate on the more complex needs of more vulnerable young people. Such services generally collaborate with other services to assist, for example young people who have been in social work care, or who have been abused, or who have problems with drug use or mental health. Direct access hostels and day centres may play a key role. Part of the information and advice they offer relates to access to accommodation and related support.

5.44   Some youth homelessness services are holistic in approach. Such services see peoples' accommodation and personal support needs as interconnected and stress that it is crucial to respond to people's needs as they are presented (for example, "on the streets" or within a day centre) and in an integrated fashion. Housing may be only one of the issues which require to be addressed[14].

5.45   Some agencies emphasised that a significant number of homeless young people have mental health needs, resulting either from prior experience of abuse, from drug and alcohol use, or from their experience of homelessness. They may have no feelings of self-worth, be depressed and have no idea where to go for help with accommodation or support services; they regularly distrust officialdom, including social workers, whom they often associate with residential care.

5.46   A further issue highlighted by homelessness agencies was the regularity with which they are required to respond to the needs of young people who have been in care. Under the Children Act 1989, local authorities have a responsibility to work in partnership with other agencies to plan to meet the needs, and to co-ordinate and fund required services, for young people leaving care and those who are vulnerable in terms of the Act. Whilst there was evidence of increased joint planning emerging in some local authority areas, there was also very clear evidence of continuing gaps and problems.

5.47   A number of initiatives have been developed which seek to promote the education of young people about housing and homelessness. Shelter and other voluntary agencies and some housing departments have tried to raise the profile of housing issues within the school system. There was evidence, however, that such initiatives have had funding difficulties.

---

14. Hutson, S. & Liddiard, M. (1994) *Youth Homelessness: The Construction of a Social Issue*, Macmillan Press; Thornton, R. (1990) *The New Homeless: The Crisis Of Youth Homelessness And The Response Of The Local Authority Housing Authorities*, SHAC.

Lesbians and gay men

5.48 Lesbians and gay men can face particular housing problems, such as finding themselves homeless at a young age because their parents do not accept their sexuality. Later, lesbians and gay men may have difficulties in establishing their rights to their home in the event of relationship breakdown or bereavement. Gay men are reported as being discriminated against when applying for a mortgage, as a result of the assumptions made about their risk of HIV/AIDS by lenders and insurance companies. However, it has been suggested that housing problems are often compounded by a lack of understanding by advice workers.[15] These needs have been recognised in the work of the London Lesbian and Gay Switchboard which receives many housing enquiries.[16]

Complex needs

5.49 Discussion of the role of housing advice services for particular client groups can easily neglect the interconnections between needs. Housing information and advice needs for the groups discussed above are not mutually exclusive. Housing advice workers regularly referred in the interviews to more complex housing information and advice needs. They described how a client with a housing problem may have both a physical disability and a learning disability; how an older person resident in a high rise block may develop a health problem; or how a homeless household may present with a variety of needs, for example a woman fleeing violence with a child with a learning disability.

5.50 One example of how an agency provides housing advice as part of a package of services for a group with more complex needs was found in a London case study (Figure 5.2). The service is typical of the more proactive services which are emerging within the voluntary and statutory sectors (sometimes in partnership) to address the more complex needs of vulnerable groups of single homeless people and other groups with care needs.

Figure 5.2   London Connection

London Connection provides a welcoming, but purposeful centre where homeless young people can go for services ranging from a cup of coffee to intensive counselling. A small minority of the young people are under 16 years, whilst around half have previously been in local authority care. Some are self-referred, others are contacted by the streetwork project, or are referred by the local authority, other youth homelessness or youth work services, or the police. Some young people have been on the streets for weeks or months and have a variety of problems. The Streetwork and Mental Health team workers say it often takes time before some homeless young people have the trust and confidence to even visit the centre; and when they have got past that hurdle, it can take longer until they disclose issues such as prior abuse. The majority of homeless young people are young men and there has been a significant growth in homelessness amongst young black people. A range of activities, including an art room and drama and music sessions are available. There are both Men's and Women's Groups and Groups of young black people, and gays and lesbians. Support is provided to pregnant young women and through a specialist project for young mothers. There is a ground floor cafe; medical services are on offer; there is a clothes store; and donated household equipment is available. Advice is available on housing and other issues, and a resettlement team, funded through the Rough Sleepers' Initiative, is also based in the Centre. Educational and training services include literacy classes, and certificated courses in skills such as computing.

---

15. Barratt, M. (1988) 'Advising Lesbians And Gay Men' in *Roof*, November pp.38-40.
16. Dibblin, J. (1988) 'Jenny Lives With Eric & Martin (And Rachael And Tracey And Kingsley And Isaac And Anwar ...)' in *Roof*, November pp.25-27.

How are clients served?
Access to advice services

5.51   Many agencies reported that a variety of factors influenced client expectations of housing advice services, of the help they could obtain and of the best routes to obtaining advice. First, the individual seeking advice will have made some assessment of his or her current circumstances and problems and of the opportunities for alleviating these, but this assessment may not be the same as the assessment an advice worker would reach. Second, individuals with housing problems vary in their knowledge and understanding of the system of advice provision and the accessibility of housing advice services, and this may lead the client to approach one particular agency, through ignorance of the existence of others, through preference if they feel intimidated, distrustful or uncomfortable in other agencies, or through choice, in an attempt to find one agency that offers an easy remedy. This leads many agencies to seek to maximise knowledge of other agencies' work, and their own accessibility. Networks between agencies and clients are considered in the next chapter, while the remainder of this chapter considers aspects of accessibility.

Publicity

5.52   Most services rely on clients to make the first approach. It is vital therefore that people who need the service are able to know it exists, and one way of ensuring that is through publicity. Local authorities with a housing advice service often used a variety of methods to publicise it. The most popular (87%) was asking other agencies to refer clients. Second most popular was the use of posters and leaflets. Council newsletters were also fairly widely used. Using the local media was popular only with authorities with advice centres (67%) or sections (63%).

5.53   In case study and other interviews, authorities varied in the extent to which they were concerned about publicity and accessibility. Generally they used several methods related to the contact officers had with other agencies and professionals in touch with potential clients. These methods included informal or formal contact with other advice agencies; writing to community groups or sending them leaflets about the advice service; and provision of training on housing issues to professionals, such as social and health workers, who may refer clients to the advice service in future. These methods were not costly, except perhaps in staff time. The location and appearance of premises can in itself act as a form of advertisement. For example, in Brighton the local authority housing advice centre is centrally located in the ground floor of council offices next to the town hall, and with prominent lettering advertising the advice centre outside. It was also publicised in a variety of literature produced by the council. In another borough, the council's housing advice centre was felt to be convenient for some parts of the borough but not all. There was a particular concern that ethnic minority groups were not using the centre as much as they might, due partly to its location.

5.54   Voluntary organisations surveyed were just as likely to publicise their housing advice service in some way, although this varied from all agencies in London to three quarters operating in districts. At least two thirds of each type of agency publicised their services: all housing advice agencies and specialist advice agencies and eight out of ten (80%) of the general advice agencies. Methods of publicity favoured posters and leaflets (93%) and referrals (90%) over the local media, which only just over four in ten (42%) used. In some case study interviews staff expressed reservations about trying to gain more publicity because they feared they could not cope with any increased demand.

Premises and facilities

5.55   Local authority housing advice services were asked a number of questions about the nature of the premises they operated from and the facilities provided. Some authorities wished to create a housing advice service that was seen as separate from the housing department, and so authorities were asked about their housing advice service reception arrangements.

5.56   Arrangements vary, largely as a consequence of the nature of the advice service. Authorities with advice centres separate from their housing departments and separate housing advice sections within their housing departments were far more likely to have different reception locations and staff from the housing department than authorities where advice was carried out from within other sections or by people with other responsibilities (Table 5.3).

5.57 Given the distribution of such advice centres and sections, this meant that the majority of inner London Boroughs (63%) and metropolitan councils (65%) reported different reception locations and staff from the housing department. In contrast, a majority of outer London boroughs (58%) and district councils (71%) used the same reception staff and locations as their housing departments. A few authorities (4) reported a separate advice centre which nonetheless shares the same reception location and staff as the housing department. It is not clear what makes such services a "centre" rather than a "service" or "section" (Table 5.3).

5.58 When asked how their premises might be described, most (65%) said they used a centrally-located office, which in most cases was part of a building which includes other council offices (47% overall). Almost three in ten (29%) use decentralised council offices, and more than one in ten (15%) describe their premises as a "shop". Seven in ten (70%) said their advice service operated from the same building as the housing department. This was least likely to be the case in metropolitan authorities and inner London boroughs where housing advice services are more likely to be described as "separate centres" or "separate sections" than in the district councils and outer London boroughs (Table 5.3).

5.59 Voluntary organisations used a variety of premises, and in case studies were more likely to report problems with finding suitable premises. Half (50%) said that they operated from a central office. One in six (17%) described themselves as operating from shop premises. This represents almost one third of the specialist advice services (31%) and one quarter (25%) of the housing advice services (Table 5.4). A quarter (26%) said that they were based in a building which included other voluntary organisations, although this was the case for only one inner London agency. Sharing premises was felt to bring advantages of economies of scale and greater contact with each other to voluntary organisations, as well as having benefits to clients who may visit more than one agency in one journey.

Table 5.3	Reception arrangement for local authority housing advice services (percentages)				
Reception Arrangement	Separate Centre	Separate Section	Separate Staff	Part of Staff Duties	All
Sample number	12	28	10	20	70
	%	%	%	%	%
Same reception, place and staff as housing department	33	36	90	70	53
Same reception place as housing department but different staff	0	14	10	5	8
Different place, different staff	67	46	0	20	35
Other	0	4	0	0	3

Source: *Telephone survey*

Table 5.4	Premises used by voluntary organisations who offer housing advice (percentages)				
	Housing Aid	Other Specialist Advice	General Advice	Social Welfare Agencies	All
Sample number	16	16	66	43	141
	%	%	%	%	%
Central office	63	63	55	38	50
Decentralised office	6	6	8	23	12
Includes council office	0	0	9	7	6
Includes other voluntary organisations	19	19	30	26	26
Shared with another	25	13	9	5	10
Shop premises	25	31	18	7	17
Day centre	0	0	9	14	9
Night shelter	0	0	0	19	3

Source: *Postal survey*

Physical access

5.60   Physical access to housing advice premises can be a problem for some clients, including wheelchair users, parents with very young children and babies, and many older people. Many if not most clients will not have a car, and so the issue of accessibility by public transport is also important. In case study visits it was apparent that virtually all agencies had an awareness of these issues, but sometimes lack of resources had prevented better provision being made. More than one local authority advice centre had undertaken capital improvements to their premises with a view to improving physical accessibility, amongst other objectives. Overall, the impression created was that voluntary organisations - with some exceptions - had relatively less suitable premises than local authorities. This mainly reflected their lack of resources. While many local authorities had premises in the heart of their built up area, many voluntary organisations commented on the tensions between cost, and finding suitable office premises close to shops, public transport, and other facilities. One voluntary aid centre was based in office premises at a distance of about quarter of a mile from the town centre, but clients had to climb a relatively tall and steep flight of stairs to gain access. In contrast the local authority advice centre in the centre of the same town was at ground floor level, with no obstacles or threshold for wheelchairs or pushchairs to overcome, and with a markedly more spacious and better-furnished waiting area.

5.61   This impression was confirmed by the results of the surveys, which revealed local authorities' premises to be more accessible than voluntary organisations' premises to people with physical disabilities. Three quarters of local authorities (75%) said their premises offered full access for physically disabled people, and a further one in six (17%) said that some of their premises offered such access. Fewer than one in ten (8%) said they had no access. In contrast, only just over two fifths (42%) of voluntary organisations said that they could offer full access for physically disabled people, over a third (36%) said that some of their premises were accessible, and more than one in five (23%) had no premises accessible to disabled people. Lack of access to premises does not necessarily make it impossible for disabled people to use advice services (see 5.66), but it adds to the cost of service delivery.

5.62   In relation to public transport, the differences between the local authority and voluntary sectors was not as great. Clients may not agree with these judgements, if the agency is based in a town centre and the client lives at some distance requiring money for bus fares, or long journeys, for example. Nine out of ten local authorities (89%) and almost as high a proportion of voluntary organisations (83%) reported convenient access to all their premises by public transport.

Opening hours

5.63   Local authority housing advice services are generally open five days a week during office hours, and in less than two in ten cases (18%) for less than 30 hours. More than half (53%) are open between 30 and 40 hours. Fewer than one in ten local authorities (9%) are open at weekends or during the evening. Voluntary agencies are somewhat more likely to provide a service on evenings or weekends: almost three in ten (29%) were open to personal callers, and almost one quarter (23%) for telephone advice. One in ten of those surveyed (12%) offers housing advice to personal callers for more than 40 hours a week, and one in ten is open for less than ten hours a week (12%). Generalist advice agencies opened for longer hours than housing advice or other specialist advice services.

5.64   The opening hours of local authority advice services appear to be related to two factors: staff numbers, and the nature of the service provided. Those which provide a case work service involving counselling and practical assistance are more likely, it seemed, from the case studies, to restrict hours so that staff can engage in the follow up work required on behalf of clients. Services which concentrate on the provision of straightforward information and advice are able to be available during normal office hours to deal with whoever seeks advice each day. In these services it seems that there is likely to be more variation in the level of service provided, depending on how busy the office is on a particular day, whereas the more intensive casework services try to provide a standard type and quality of service to all clients. This was apparent also in the voluntary sector.

5.65   Some agencies who provide advice are accessible at times other than normal office hours, when unexpected homelessness usually occurs. Nearly all local authorities provide emergency homelessness services on a 24 hour basis.[17] Other services in the voluntary and local authority sectors are designed to reach people who are unlikely to approach traditional office-based services.

Methods of accessibility

5.66   Although local authority housing advice services are generally office-based, they may deliver a service in ways which do not require the client to attend an office, such as through home visits. In addition other local authority services such as outreach social work services to hostels, tenancy relations services, and welfare benefits advice, may be delivered away from an office base. All local authority housing advice services were accessible by telephone, and all but one by personal visit with no appointment and by written correspondence. Nine out of ten (90%) provided home visits in certain circumstances. Three quarters (76%) would arrange appointments in advance for clients, and two thirds (69%) would arrange appointments in advance with referral agencies. These proportions did not vary much from one type of service to another or from one authority type to another.

5.67   Voluntary organisations were also available to clients in a number of ways. Over eight in ten (83%) could be accessed by personal visit without appointment, and a higher number (94%) offer advice by telephone. Three quarters (76%) provide home visits in some circumstances. A telephone advice service has been developed by Shelter and other agencies in Lincolnshire, a large rural area. Only one in ten voluntary organisations could offer clients a freephone facility, and half of these were generalist advice agencies. Very few of the agencies used a mobile van or streetwork to take advice services to the client. In practice, though, some agencies may not be as accessible as these results overall suggest. For example, some are very hard to contact by telephone. To prevent this, CABx in one metropolitan area entered into a service level agreement with the council which required the telephones to be answered within a specified time.

---

17. Mullins, D. & Niner, P. with Marsh, A. & Walker, B. (1996) *Evaluation of the 1991 Homelessness Code of Guidance*, London, HMSO.

5.68   Some groups are less likely to seek help directly from office-based advice services, it was felt by some voluntary organisations. They may find it an uncomfortable atmosphere for receiving advice.[18] This has been recognised in the design of certain services. Agencies in London and elsewhere have developed a variety of telephone advice services and nightlines, outreach, streetwork and resettlement services in order to improve access to advice, and emergency accommodation particularly for homeless young people and people sleeping rough. Day centres, for hostel residents and people who are sleeping rough, may also provide advice on benefits, accommodation options, follow on support options, specialist support and health services.

5.69   In urban areas, where there are many social and private landlords, as well as more agencies providing advice, access to the right advice service therefore plays an important role in influencing outcomes. For those in rural districts, where there are fewer landlords, access to information and advice about options may be very restricted.

Translation and interpretation

5.70   Accessibility to advice for people who do not speak English requires interpretation and translation services. There were wide variations between different types of local authority in the extent to which these are available, with all London boroughs and nine out of ten metropolitan councils (89%) saying that some or all premises offer translation and interpretation for minority languages, whereas fewer than half the district councils (45%) do. Just over half (52%) of the voluntary organisations and almost six in ten (59%) of the housing aid centres said that they could offer interpretation and translation in all or some of their premises. Organisations which provide services for homeless people are least likely (34%) to be able to offer this sort of service. The point was made during case study interviews that help could often be provided only if the agency was made aware in advance of the need for translation.

Privacy

5.71   Clients who do not have privacy when they speak to housing advisers may feel inhibited in their conversation with them, and so reduce their own access to appropriate information and advice. Local authorities were all able to provide private interviewing facilities in some advice premises, and only three per cent could not do so in all advice premises. A slightly smaller proportion of voluntary organisations (88%) could provide this facility in all their premises, and only two agencies were unable to offer any private space. This may overstate the use of private space: one case study accommodation agency had an open plan office with three desks in shop premises, in which clients were expected to discuss their case, while sitting across the desk from the adviser. In theory, the agency had private space upstairs, but it was not routinely offered and would have been inaccessible to some clients.

Summary

5.72   This chapter has answered a number of questions about the clients of housing advice services. There was general consensus about the needs to be met by housing advice services, with most agencies in both sectors concentrating on the most vulnerable in social and economic terms, and especially on homeless and potentially homeless people, although most also make their services available to anyone. Voluntary organisations were more clearly divided into two groups: those who target their services at specific groups, and those who provide services for everyone. Little can be said systematically overall about who uses the services, although individual agencies may have monitoring systems in use. Local authorities with dedicated advice centres and sections were most likely to have such systems, along with some voluntary organisations, especially those who are members of a national network. Specialist services for particular needs seem to have

18. Thornton, R. (1990) *The New Homeless: The Crisis Of Youth Homelessness And The Response Of The Local Authority Housing Authorities*, SHAC; Randall, G. & Brown, S. 1994 *Falling Out: A Research Study Of Homeless Ex-Service People*, Crisis.

expanded in recent years, for a variety of reasons, and these often involve statutory and voluntary sectors working together. Agencies are generally concerned to ensure accessibility to their services, and this has been reflected in high proportions with easy access for people with physical disabilities, for example. Overall, local authorities tended to have more suitable and accessible premises, opening hours and facilities such as translation and interpretation, but the key difference in the latter case was between urban and more rural authorities. Overall, in the local authority sector, authorities with dedicated advice centres and sections, found especially in London boroughs and metropolitan authorities, had the clearest idea of who they aimed to serve, who they were reaching, and how they should be accessible. No such clear pattern emerged in the voluntary sector, with most agencies' strong commitment to physical accessibility qualified by resource constraints.

6 Networks and Collaboration

6.1   Previous chapters have touched on how agencies work together to provide services and how recent policy developments, such as promoting the enabling role of housing authorities, and care in the community, require agencies to collaborate. This chapter examines the role of networks and collaboration between housing advice agencies, social welfare agencies which provide advice, and clients. It describes national and local networks which play a role in housing advice services, and it considers the conditions for effective collaboration in the development and delivery of services. It is organised in two main parts, which are concerned with formal structures, and the working arrangements which bring workers, clients and agencies together.

Defining 'network'

6.2   "Network" is used here to refer to *a pattern of working relationships and links* between individuals and agencies, which may have developed for a number of reasons, such as in dealing with clients' problems, or discussing policy developments, and which may be more or less formalised in forums, for example. The existence of such links, even if only in the form of knowing of each other's presence, was demonstrated in several areas by directories of names and addresses of advice agencies, and by collaboration between advisers in different agencies about individual cases. This definition is wider than the use of network to refer to *the formal structures* which arise when agencies and advice workers combine together for a common purpose, for example, to provide support services such as training or expertise, or to consider the issue of youth homelessness. Such formal networks can be a useful way of developing collaboration, but are not a substitute for it.

6.3   Where agencies involved in providing housing advice in one local authority area do not have any contact, or even know of each other's existence, it is more appropriate to describe this as a *latent* network. In some districts there is evidence that agencies lack knowledge about each others' roles, and may have difficulties or blocks in communication. For example, there is no certainty that housing department and local CAB staff will ever have met.

6.4   Networks are not mutually exclusive. Agencies may participate in more than one, at local, regional and national levels, and in different activities, for example, referral, and policy development. Participation may be either formal (based on written policies, or formal membership of federated organisations, for example) or informal. Networks may be internal to an agency or be formed between different agencies or service sector boundaries; or they may be both internal and external to a particular agency, for example, forums which bring people together from several departments of a local authority and from other agencies.

National advice organisations

6.5   National voluntary organisations such as NACAB, CHAR (the "housing campaign for single people") and Shelter playing a key role in the development and delivery of advice services at national and local level were described in Chapter 4. Generally, their work has some common strands, although they differ greatly in how they are organised; in the number of members they have, with NACAB largest with over 700 members; in what they do; and in the resources they have available to them. In common they have the objective of linking together a number of local voluntary sector providers of advice services, and providing services to them. Some raise and disburse funds for local centres. At national level they have a role as campaigning organisations on issues affecting their own networks of advice agencies, and on policy issues affecting their clients, called "social policy work" by NACAB. Some or all of them come together in the Advice Services Alliance and elsewhere to consider common issues, to develop services jointly, to consider new opportunities such as the introduction of legal aid funding for non-solicitor advice agencies, and to lobby policy makers on advice and policy issues.

6.6   Examples of their work include CHAR's Day Centres Project, providing support for day centres serving single homeless people throughout the country. Some also have a direct role in advice provision, for example, Shelter's Nightline, and CHAS's central London Housing Aid Centre. Some, such as NACAB, receive grants from central government departments in recognition of their role in supporting advice throughout the country, and some are reliant on a combination of members' fees, earnings from services and charitable donations from individuals, companies, and trusts. Some operate conditions for membership, as in NACAB's reviews of the work of each member CAB every three years. Others, such as CHAR, operate an open membership policy.

6.7   The National Homelessness Advisory Service involves a partnership between NACAB and Shelter. It was established in 1990 with funding from the Department of the Environment through section 73 of the Housing Act 1985. The aims are to help prevent and relieve homelessness by the provision of good quality advice within CABx and independent advice centres, using the specialist knowledge of Shelter. The service has developed in phases, and is available to a majority of CABx, and since 1995 it has been available to some of FIAC's members. The service involves basing a worker in a local Shelter aid centre to provide information, training, referral and consultancy services to a number of local advice centres. One illustration of its work is given in Figure 6.1.

Figure 6.1   National Homelessness Advisory Service

National Homelessness Advisory Service in Tyneside

Tyneside Housing Aid Centre (THAC) was a founder member of the NHAS in 1990. CAB enquiries to THAC on housing and homelessness matters have increased significantly and around 200 staff and volunteers have been trained. Two staff provide consultancy and training for 29 Citizens Advice Bureaux (CABx) as well as some case work assistance for their clients. Much of the work is on the telephone. In 1994/95 a total of 439 CABx workers were trained, and THAC staff, using the consultancy helpline, assisted CABx staff to help resolve a housing problem for a client on 590 occasions. Whilst THAC provides housing advice through the CABx, it believes that the relationship is productive for THAC in that it often refers complex benefits issues to the CAB.

Local forums

6.8   At the local level there are many examples of different types of forums which bring people and organisations together. Some of these are confined to the statutory sector, some to the voluntary sector, and many involve people from both sectors and sometimes from the private sector also. They vary from formal membership organisations, with constitutions and resources of their own, to informal meetings held at regular or irregular intervals. One example of such a forum, the Homeless Network in London, is provided in Figure 6.2. Sometimes new services develop from the work of such forums, and are managed by one, or more than one, of the agencies involved. An example of such a service is provided in Figure 6.3.

Homeless Network - London

This federation, formed in 1973, operates as an alliance of voluntary agencies working to improve services for single homeless people in London. The Network has a remit to co-ordinate strategies, encourage collaboration in service delivery and provide services such as information and training to member agencies. It co-ordinates the work of member agencies in relation to the Rough Sleepers Initiative. It has 22 members and nine associates. A meeting on housing advice led to a checklist of issues and a useful summary of advice services was produced, which lists telephone and specialist advice agencies for homeless people in London, and other details of the availability of many specialist advice services.

Figure 6.3   A local service provided by voluntary and statutory organisations

Heckmondwike Advice Shop

This shop provides advice services to people in the Heckmondwike area of Kirklees (West Yorkshire). Regular surgeries are provided by five agencies, and another two will visit by appointment. The lead agency was the Kirklees CHAS Housing Aid Centre, and they and Age Concern, the CAB, the Racial Equality Council and the Careers Service provide regular surgeries. The Benefits Advice Service of Kirklees Council and the Community Health Council visit by appointment. The advice shop is managed in a partnership between Kirklees CHAS, the CAB, Age Concern, and the Benefits Advice Service.

Local authority perceptions

6.9   Local authorities reported high levels of contact between agencies involved in advice provision. Three quarters of authorities (75%) said representatives of advice agencies came together to discuss matters of common concern (Table 6.1). Of these, seven in ten (70%) said that new services, policies or agencies had resulted. Some officers commented that it was not always easy to trace the origins of a new development to one forum. Fewer than half (46%) said there were co-ordinating agencies in their area involved in homelessness services, although in metropolitan areas the proportion was two thirds (67%). Only just over half (53%) of authorities with no identifiable housing advice service reported contact between advice agencies compared with over eight in ten (83%) of remaining authorities.

Table 6.1   Perceptions by local authorities of local forums and their activities (percentages)

Forum Activity	Type of Authority			All Authorities
	London Boroughs	Metropolitan Councils	District Councils	
Sample number	21	22	58	101
	%	%	%	%
Co-ordinating agency or forum (homelessness)	48	67	38	46
Local forum (involving agencies)	70	86	71	75

Source: *Telephone survey*

Voluntary organisations' perceptions

6.10   Seven in ten voluntary organisations (71%) knew of ways in which representatives of advice services came together, almost as high a proportion as for local authorities. And almost six in ten (57%) of these knew of new services, policies or agencies developing from them. General advice agencies were less likely than any other type of agency to know of a forum, with just under two thirds (64%) saying they know of one. Over eight in ten (83%) housing aid centres, a similar proportion (80%) of specialist advice agencies, and three quarters (74%) of social welfare agencies knew of a forum.

Both sectors

6.11 Authorities and voluntary organisations reported coming together with others for a number of specific reasons, and the main focus was rarely advice provision alone. More commonly the focus was on client groups such as private tenants, young homeless people, and other "special needs" groups; or on policies such as care in the community and private sector housing. In Kirklees, senior staff of the housing department and the CHAS housing aid centre meet quarterly, a rare example of such a forum focusing on housing advice services. Forums may be organised in an ad hoc way, meeting irregularly in various locations, or they may be more formally convened and serviced by one of the agencies involved, perhaps the local authority, as in the Brighton Private Sector Housing Forum, see Figure 6.4.

Figure 6.4   A private sector housing forum, serviced by the council

Brighton Private Sector Housing Forum

The Forum was established in 1992, at the borough's initiative. It is serviced by the housing department, a significant workload for one officer. It meets bi-monthly, with meetings of an elected steering group bi-monthly as well. It has agreed terms of reference and is chaired by a senior councillor. The director of the Brighton Housing Trust chairs the steering group. Membership is open to all who "have an interest in, or are involved in delivering or receiving private sector housing services in Brighton and Hove". It has been the leading actor in initiatives such as a model rent book for assured tenancies; an empty property strategy; the production of *The good landlord guide*, written jointly by the council's private sector team and the Housing Trust's Housing Advice and Legal Centre; and the development of an accredited private landlords scheme.

Working arrangements

6.12 Formal structures such as forums may assist joint working, but they will not guarantee good working relationships. What may appear to be a good organisational working relationship may depend on a relationship established between individual officers and so may be vulnerable to staff change, unless the right conditions exist for new staff also to establish good relations with others. Four different types of working arrangement can be detected, concerned with:

- referral and consultation processes between agencies in relation to clients;

- relationships between "specialist" and "generalist" services;

- relationships between primary and secondary services;

- joint service provision and planning.

6.13 These are not mutually exclusive categories. For example, in the course of assisting one client, an adviser in a "generalist" agency may consult an expert in another "specialist" agency, illustrating the first two types of working arrangement. There may be formal agreements on how liaison should operate, but the importance of informal arrangements needs to be recognised - for example, the informal approach one advice worker might make to another in a different agency in seeking expert help with a particularly difficult problem.

Referrals, consultation and case work

6.14 As Chapter 5 showed, people's housing problems do not necessarily manifest themselves in neat packages, and even if they did, clients would not necessarily know which agency to approach. So referrals between agencies inevitably take place, from one voluntary agency to another, and from statutory to voluntary organisations, and vice versa. Lack of knowledge by one agency of the role and expertise of other agencies will impede the delivery of the best available advice services in particular circumstances.

6.15   In both voluntary and local authority sectors an important distinction can be made between referral of clients to another agency, and consultation, where an agency might seek specialist advice, for example, from a law centre, in order to handle a case itself. The latter indicates a model of service delivery which stresses the adviser's role in drawing on expertise as necessary from within or outside the agency, and, if appropriate, arranging a case conference.

6.16   Local authorities and voluntary organisations were asked about their referral patterns and policies. The results are presented in Tables 6.2 and 6.3. They need to be interpreted with care, since what appears to be a low referral rate may reflect the fact that no agency such as a law centre exists within reasonable reach of the client. Also, the tables cannot indicate how often referrals take place, nor how they take place. However, they provide an indication of the perceptions of housing authorities about the range of agencies that exist to which they might refer clients, and from which clients are referred. Referrals may be governed by formal agreements or less formal understandings about organisations' roles, but more commonly referrals operate informally.

6.17   Generally metropolitan and London authorities were more likely to refer to other agencies than district authorities, and authorities with dedicated advice staff and services were more likely to refer than others. The most common referral reported by (96%) local authorities is to CABx. Almost two thirds of local authorities (63% overall and 57% of district councils) say they refer to voluntary sector housing aid centres, a result which might look surprising given the distribution of Shelter, CHAS and other centres in England. It seems likely that authorities are referring clients to housing aid centres based in some other town or local authority area, in some cases at some distance. Authorities with housing aid centres of their own were least likely to say they referred people to independent HACs. Half the authorities with advice centres separate from the housing department refer to law centres, whereas only one in five (19%) of those with no identifiable advice service did so. Referrals to welfare benefits or rights advice were very common (63% of authorities); Care and Repair or Staying Put schemes were also frequently mentioned (by 62% of authorities), as were accommodation agencies (75%), and the same proportion mentioned supported accommodation. Large proportions also mentioned solicitors (82%), estate agents (72%), and building societies (58%) (Table 6.2).

6.18   Voluntary organisations reported some similar patterns of referrals, but smaller proportions reported referral to most agencies (Table 6.3). This possibly reflects the greater likelihood that some voluntary organisations will provide a counselling and case-work service for their clients, or refer to other expertise on behalf of their clients. By far the largest referral rate was to local authority homelessness units, which nine in ten (91%) of organisations reported. Second most frequently mentioned, by two in three voluntary organisations (66%) were voluntary sector housing aid centres. Nearly three quarters (73%) of the general advice agencies mentioned such referrals. Law centres were mentioned by almost half (46%) as referral destinations, but relatively few voluntary organisations (30%) operating in district council areas reported such referrals, so reflecting the lack of law centres outside large urban areas in England. As with local authorities, voluntary organisations reported many referrals to agencies which provide wider services to people in housing difficulty. Almost nine in ten (87%) reported referring people to solicitors, half (49%) refer to accommodation agencies, and over half (54%) to supported accommodation.

6.19   Authorities and voluntary organisations were also asked who referred people to them (Tables 6.2 and 6.3). Broadly their answers reflected a similar picture of referrals, with all but one authority saying they received referrals from CAB, and four out of five (80%) saying they received referrals from voluntary sector housing aid centres. Similar proportions of district and metropolitan authorities (77% and 76% respectively) said they received referrals from such housing aid centres, but the volume of referrals is not reported. High proportions of authorities reported receiving referrals from solicitors (86%), building societies (73%), and supported accommodation projects (63%) (Table 6.2).

Table 6.2	Local authority referrals to and from other services (percentages)			
Services Referred To/From	Type of Authority			All Authorities
	London Boroughs	Metropolitan Councils	District Councils	
Sample number	23/23	22/22	60/58	105/103
	%	%	%	%
CAB	96/96	96/100	97/100	96/99
Solicitors	100/96	86/82	73/85	82/86
Voluntary housing aid centre	83/91	59/77	57/76	63/80
Supported accommodation	78/70	91/68	65/59	73/63
Building societies	52/83	50/68	63/71	58/73
Accommodation agencies	83/0	41/9	80/27	75/48
Estate agents	74/48	73/36	72/47	72/45
Welfare benefits or rights	65/52	82/68	52/43	63/51
Care and Repair or Staying Put	74/61	64/46	53/40	62/46
Specialist support services	83/61	73/77	40/38	56/52
Night shelter	83/57	55/46	43/35	54/42
Day centre	52/40	64/64	32/35	43/44
Tenancy relations service	57/52	59/56	23/21	38/34
Money advice: non-statutory sector	26/26	41/27	28/21	31/23
Law centre	61/52	55/59	12/10	31/30
Money advice: public sector	30/26	41/14	20/21	27/20

Source: *Telephone survey*

6.20   More voluntary organisations (84%) said they received referrals from CAB than from any other source. Next most frequently mentioned (by 74% of voluntary organisations) was local authority homeless units, followed by "other local authority" (72%) and solicitors (70% of voluntary organisations). Least mentioned were Care and Repair or Staying Put projects (mentioned by 23% of organisations), tenancy relations services (30% of organisations) and estate agents (26%) (Table 6.3).

6.21   How these referral patterns arise and operate was of interest and local authorities and voluntary organisations were asked if they had referral policies. Fewer than half the authorities (37%) said they had referrals policies, and even fewer could supply one on paper but officers said they often had an informal understanding with other agencies about the sort of case that they would refer elsewhere. Within local government there were clear guidelines or expectations, whether written down or not, for example about the relative roles of homelessness and advice services where they both exist, but at times the case studies revealed that agencies had slightly different understandings about each others roles, or that they knew exactly how they were supposed to behave, but acted differently in the interests of the client, for example, in referring people to additional or independent sources of assistance.

6.22   Voluntary organisations were less likely (28%) to have a referral policy, and, as with local authorities, very few could supply one on paper. In interviews, however, staff had no difficulty saying what their understanding of referral processes was, and sometimes to report unwritten agreements.

6.23   Voluntary organisations were also asked how referrals generally take place and whether staff are trained in the procedures to use. Over two thirds (67%) of the voluntary organisations said they are trained. The most frequently used type of referral (reported by 80% of organisations) was making an appointment while the client was there. Over seven out of ten (74%) reported telling clients where to go. Over half (53%) reported that they sometimes arranged an appointment for a client then told the client the details later, and the same number (53%) said they sometimes asked other agencies to notify the client of an appointment. Organisations reported an average of almost three types of referral procedure, indicating a degree of flexibility and confirming what many interviewees in case studies said about treating each case separately and doing whatever seemed best in the circumstances of the case.

Table 6.3	Voluntary organisations' referrals to and from other services (percentages)				
Services Referred To/From	Housing Advice Service Type				All
	Housing Aid	Specialist Advice	General Advice	Social Welfare Agencies	
Sample number	18/17	15/16	66/64	44/44	143/141
	%	%	%	%	%
Homelessness unit or officer	94/84	92/63	87/64	89/84	91/74
Solicitors	83/94	80/81	94/83	79/39	87/70
Citizens Advice Bureau	89/100	80/94	29/45	91/79	60/84
Other local authority	72/77	60/81	53/70	57/68	57/72
Local authority advice service or centre	33/65	47/94	58/67	61/59	55/69
Voluntary sector housing aid sector	56/59	60/50	73/33	55/54	66/56
Decentralised housing office	83/94	53/69	55/44	59/54	59/56
Specialist support services	50/59	47/56	56/34	75/68	60/50
Welfare benefits or rights centre	44/59	47/56	32/44	77/50	49/61
Supported accommodation	72/71	27/38	38/22	79/70	54/45
Day centres	61/59	13/38	32/52	52/52	40/51
Night shelter	67/59	27/19	53/31	54/45	52/38
Law centre	44/47	27/38	36/28	66/32	46/41
Money advice centre - non-statutory sector	61/53	47/31	33/34	43/20	41/39
Accommodation agencies	67/53	13/6	52/22	50/36	49/28
Tenancy relations service	61/47	53/38	46/31	29/23	43/30
Money advice centre - public sector	22/29	40/56	18/27	36/18	27/39
Building societies	22/12	0/25	36/63	14/9	24/36
Estate agents	39/24	7/25	36/36	29/11	32/26
Care and Repair/Staying Put	50/24	13/13	30/20	16/14	27/23

Source: *Postal survey*

6.24   Another indication of the relationships between agencies was provided when they were asked about the availability of advice from specialist staff, and training and participation in local networks. Over eight in ten local authorities (85%) reported the availability of advice and support from specialist staff such as welfare rights officers or social workers to at least some of their advice staff. It is perhaps surprising that any did not report such support, given the skills available to every local authority. One case study authority's welfare benefits unit reported not using the council's legal staff for specialist advice because they were not felt to have the right skills, and because a service level agreement was not affordable to the unit. In this case the staff had informal access to the staff of a law centre so met their need that way. Almost two thirds of authorities (65%) reported that all staff were trained on local networks of advice and support services. Six in ten reported that some staff attended or contributed to inter-agency forums, and a further 32 per cent reported that all staff did so.

6.25   Voluntary organisations reported higher rates of contact between some or all their of staff and specialist staff (79 and 13% reporting all and some staff), higher rates of training in local networks (73 and 20%), and very slightly higher levels of participation in inter-agency forums (53 and 43%). For all three indicators the proportion was at least 90 per cent reporting that at least some staff took part.

Relationships between "specialist" and "generalist" services

6.26   A distinction is often drawn between "generalist" advice agencies such as CABx which aim to serve any member of the public with any sort of problem, and agencies which specialise, say, in housing or legal advice. Relationships between them can show a complicated pattern of consultation in several directions over casework and other issues. For example, a CAB may consult a housing aid centre over a housing enquiry, and be consulted by the housing aid centre about another enquiry in which the CAB is known to be more expert. There was a difference detected in the case studies between agencies that saw their role as "casework" involving counselling, advice and advocacy, and others who saw their role as providers of information and advice. The latter were less likely to use the word "client" to describe enquirers, and were much more likely to tell the client to go to another agency for further assistance, perhaps making an appointment for them. In contrast, the casework agencies were more likely to bring in expertise or other agencies to assist with a case, while maintaining a lead role.

6.27   The notion that "specialist" agencies act as a back up to "generalist" agencies was not found to fit the reality of relationships and roles. In practice "specialist" and "generalist" advice agencies cannot be easily distinguished. For example, CABx are increasingly providing their own specialist services in the fields of employment, immigration, housing, money and legal advice. In any case, they are capable of dealing with many "specialist" housing or other problems even without the resources of a specialist, though that expertise is sometimes required. Also, "specialist" services such as law centres and welfare rights services often wish to maximise access, and not just through referrals from "generalist" agencies. In practice, agencies seek to minimise referral, though argue for the case for access to specialist expertise themselves, and sometimes for their clients, when necessary. Finally, people's problems do not manifest themselves necessarily in neat "general" or "specialist" forms.

Relationships between primary and secondary services

6.28   The distinction between primary - advice giving - services, and secondary - back-up - services providing training, information and other support - seems to be clearly understood by advice agencies, but in practice few organisations provide unambiguous examples of one or the other type of service. NACAB and FIAC are examples of organisations providing only secondary services.

6.29   For agencies who provide secondary as well as primary services, the balance between the two can become problematic, since the direct advice-giving role can dominate. It may be only by careful management of resources, and sometimes only by saying no to desperate clients that the secondary work can be protected. This is illustrated in Figure 6.3.

6.30   At local level, most agencies surveyed in this study were primary providers of advice, but some also provided secondary services, and this was not always clear from the agency or service name. For example, one local authority welfare rights service had made a conscious decision to limit the time available for individual casework, and did so by refusing to see clients outside the allotted times. Staff spent the rest of their time in a variety of training and development work with other agencies, for example training social workers, CAB workers and others. They felt that in the longer term their efforts would be more effective in assisting more people than if they encouraged other advice workers to believe that only they could handle welfare advice work. They and other agencies, however, said how important it was to do some casework, since it provided insights that no amount of other work could, as well as ensuring provision for the most complex cases.

6.31   Agencies which were set up as primary advice giving agencies can often see the value of more proactive secondary work as a result of the cases they handle. Some local authorities, for example, reported that they would like to do more to contact landlords and provide them with promotional material about their rights and obligations. Sometimes advice agencies were able to act on these ideas and sometimes they were not.

Figure 6.5   A local secondary and primary advice service

Shelter Merseyside - Young Persons Resource Centre

The Resource Centre was formed in 1989, primarily to co-ordinate youth homelessness and housing advice services and to provide secondary advice, training and information services for agencies serving homeless young people. As the City Council in Liverpool managed two Housing Aid Centres, Shelter took the view that a second tier role would be more appropriate. The staffing consists of a co-ordinator, a resource worker and an administrator/information worker. The steering group involves Liverpool City Council, the Social Services Department from neighbouring Sefton Borough, Liverpool University, the Young Persons Housing Association (Wirral) Farm Housing Association and two supported housing projects for young people based in St Helens and Liverpool. Despite the secondary service objectives, some agencies referred young people to the service for basic housing advice. This showed they recognised their lack of knowledge about young peoples' rights. The role, services and resources of the centre have been under review recently and the specialist casework role has been confirmed, in addition to the original role in research, training and information. Whilst casework is seen as a key function, there are concerns about the balance of the workload as casework involves immediate demands and staff resources are limited. The Centre has recently gained funding for a casework post.

6.32   Secondary agencies can play a key role in the co-ordination and development of services which involve more than one agency. For example, Homeless Network's role in the Rough Sleeping Initiative involved co-ordination of services provided by several agencies. The Network describes its role as reflecting "a common cause between the homeless network and the government, all of whom were concerned about the growth of rough sleeping in London and its implications.[1] The initiative encouraged partnerships between advice services, referral services, assessment services and accommodation services. The value of collaboration is demonstrated also in the development of a new secondary service, see Figure 6.6.

Figure 6.6   The development of a secondary service

The Money Advice Support service

This service aims to provide secondary support to money advice and debt services throughout the UK, and to improve co-ordination between them. There is an emphasis on training and information, and a desire to establish common quality standards and the most efficient use of available resources through co-ordination and co-operation. It involves all the main independent agencies which provide money advice support services: NACAB, the Birmingham Settlement, FIAC, the Money Advice Association and others. The Money Advice Support Service is substantially funded through the private sector.

---

1. Homeless Network (1994) *Annual Report 1993/94.*

6.33 A useful distinction can be drawn between joint strategic planning and joint service provision, though in practice the two may be carried out simultaneously. The case studies revealed some examples of joint service planning taking place after agencies identified a gap in services and attempted to find ways to fill it. Figure 6.7 provides an example of a service provided by collaboration amongst several voluntary and statutory agencies.

6.34 Much less common were attempts to consider overall levels of advice service provision across the authority area. However, in Scotland, the idea of local housing information and advice strategies was promoted by HomePoint, and "researching the providers" is seen as an essential early step.[2] Three case study authorities were reviewing provision, or had carried out a review in the recent past, and others were known to be doing or considering the same. In Wandsworth, a review was carried out as a result of concern about the level of spending on grants to voluntary sector advice providers. The authority decided to enter into a contract for the delivery of services, to the alarm of the voluntary sector advice agencies, several of whom combined in a consortium to bid for the housing advice contract. This sort of situation is likely to get more common, and could have a damaging effect on relationships between agencies who win contracts and those who do not - if they survive. However, those who do collaborate to win contracts may benefit from greater clarity about roles and relationships.

Figure 6.7   A joint service for homeless people

A partnership health centre - Newcastle

Homeless North, a voluntary organisation, and the National Health Service are involved in the management of the Bridge Medical Centre, located in an old morgue on the riverside. The Centre offers a range of health and support services for homeless people including access to GPs, counselling, a needle exchange and baths. It is mainly staffed by health personnel, and the administration is by Homeless North. The Centre plays a role in advising people about accommodation and services to homeless people, and refers on to specialist housing advice agencies. It is open every day, although one day is for women only. Staff do outreach work to encourage take-up. The Centre is used to the extent that the building can be overcrowded and the upstairs is not in use for safety reasons. Plans for a new base are being developed with a housing association.

Improving networks

6.35 Although the surveys and case studies revealed a high level of contact between agencies in relation to case work and some in relation to service planning, workers in the local authority and voluntary sectors said that more contact was required. They reported a number of obstacles to effective collaboration and highlighted a number of conditions which promote and constrain such collaboration. Constraints, blocks or opportunities in relation to joint work included:

● if agencies and staff are under pressure, they have limited time available to engage in networks systematically, or at all; or to develop new services such as secondary services which have longer term benefits;

● agencies may not have the staff or technology to engage in monitoring or to communicate the results to other agencies with common interests; this impedes the dissemination of information about what agencies actually do, an issue to be returned to in Chapter 8;

---

2. Palmer, J. & Gibson, P. (1996) *Local Housing Information and Advice Strategies: a Good Practice Guide*, Scottish Homes, Edinburgh.

- the presence of a clear co-ordinating role, either within the local authority or the voluntary sector, can be a significant influence on local networking; local authorities have a potential role as enablers here which is not as well developed as it could be;

- collaboration in specific circumstances such as over joint training or policy reviews can have benefits in the development of relationships which extend beyond the immediate results.

6.36   The strategies of funders play a significant role in supporting the development and effectiveness of networks, their co-ordinating role and related joint work. This was evident in a number of case study examples which receive significant funding and support from local authorities. Network effectiveness depends on a variety of support and resources. As well as financial resources, their co-ordinating activities require legitimation by the statutory agencies and other funders, as well as by their members.

6.37   The experience of joint work and relationships between agencies and workers in the field of community care suggests some additional conditions which may be equally conducive to effective joint work in the field of housing advice:

- a degree of consensus in relation to aims and strategies on the one hand, and roles on the other;

- awareness of the network and clarity about roles, rather than insularity;

- joint planning, co-ordination and joint training;

- appreciation of the differing professional value systems and their implications for practice, for example in relation to confidentiality;

- recognition that there are benefits in working together, and that no single agency can resolve problems on their own;

- trust between organisations and individuals;

- the need for time to establish and maintain systems to make communications quick, easy and automatic;

- part-time workers and volunteers have information needs that may need special attention.[3]

Summary

6.38   Collaboration between agencies involved in giving housing advice is essential to effective service delivery. This chapter has examined the formal and informal networks and working relationships which exist between agencies, and has shown high levels of contact between them, especially in relation to case-work. Referrals are rarely governed by formal agreements but many informal understandings apply. Few agencies are solely primary or secondary providers, and many generalist agencies provide some specialist services. Less contact occurs in relation to strategic planning. Some agencies in many areas meet in forums, but these rarely focus only on advice. However, such forums often assist in the development of new services including some delivered jointly.

---

3.   Hudson, B. (1987) 'Collaboration in Social Welfare: A Framework for Analysis' *Policy & Politics*, Vol 15 No 3 pp.175-182; Ovreteit, J. (1993) *Co-ordinating Community Care - Multi Disciplinary Teams and Care Management*, Open University Press.

7 Resources

7.1   This chapter describes and considers the evidence about funding sources and spending patterns for housing advice services in local authorities and the voluntary sector. The use of the title "resources" is intended to reflect a concern with the costs of running services and with the sources of income used to fund them, and is also used here in particular to encompass the staff skills and volunteers' time which agencies may bring to their advice work. The number and training of staff is considered as well as the costs and funding of advice services. Other resources, such as inter-agency forums are considered in Chapter 5.

7.2   Although resources to provide and develop services is a common concern across the voluntary and statutory sector, it proved difficult to collect systematic data about the incidence of costs and the use of resources, especially within local government. Even if fuller data were available, there could be some difficulty in interpreting it. The difficulties in defining "housing advice" lead to similar difficulties in attributing costs to "advice" and to other activities. For example, what proportion of the cost of a housing department neighbourhood office serving a council estate should be attributed to "advice"; and how many of the costs of running a day centre or holistic counselling service for young homeless people should be considered "advice" costs, and how many within that should be considered "*housing* advice" costs?

7.3   Local authorities with dedicated advice services and centres found it easier to answer these questions than others. Some authorities and voluntary organisations considered it would be unreasonable to devote time to provide more information, since it was not readily at hand. A small number were fearful that the information might be misinterpreted by funders. Overall, the costs reported are probably an under-estimate of the true costs to organisations of providing services, and also an under-estimate of the resources provided by local authorities to voluntary organisations. Further research could usefully be done to develop an agreed model for showing the costs and benefits of housing advice services.

Past patterns

7.4   The historical development of advice services helps explain the pattern of funding today. Typically advice services grew as a result of voluntary action, local authority service development, or central government initiative, with local authorities asked to contribute to voluntary and local authority costs as time-limited central government funding declined. A local authority might have started to provide grants to the citizens' advice bureaux in the 1950s or 1960s. Housing budgets would not have been expected to contribute. In the 1970s and 1980s some specialist advice services, including housing, may have started, at first on a voluntary basis, but increasingly funded by local authority and central government funds. Local authorities themselves may have opened housing advice centres, funded from their general accounts, and would have put greater emphasis on the advice role of estate management and private sector staff in the housing department. With some exceptions, authorities would not have had a strategy for funding advice services in general or housing advice in particular. This is illustrated in Figure 7.1, which describes the pattern of funding for advice services in Brighton from the early 1970s to the early 1990s, when a review was carried out.

7.5   Two factors seem significant in changing this pattern of funding. First, funding constraints arising from the tight public spending controls and the reduction in funds available from central sources, have led authorities to seek to ensure value for money and to avoid any duplication in the work of voluntary organisations they are expected to fund. Second, the introduction of new methods of management through contracts and service level agreements has begun to have an impact in the funding decisions taken in relation to housing and other advice services, though few authorities have got as far as entering into formal contracts. This trend is likely to accelerate with the introduction of a statutory duty to secure comprehensive housing advice services. More authorities are likely to develop internal financial management systems and cost centres so that they can identify more clearly the incidence of housing advice expenditure.

Local authority sources of funding

7.6   The financial costs to local authorities of providing housing advice services will never be easy to calculate because of the difficulties in defining "housing advice" which were discussed in Chapter 3. But even some local authorities with dedicated housing advice staff had difficulty in saying what were the origins of the money they spent on housing advice. This was partly a reflection of the accounting practices and division of labour of many local authorities - for example, other officers at other positions in the hierarchy, perhaps in other departments, might have been able to supply the information. It is also partly a reflection of the nature of spending - it is largely committed to salaries rather than to consumables, which require a lot of monitoring during the year. But it is a sign of how "housing advice" has not been seen as an identifiable item of expenditure that so little was known.

7.7   Authorities with identifiable housing advice services were asked about the sources of funding. The two main sources identified were the Housing Revenue Account and the council's General Account. Fewer than half were able to apportion expenditure between these two accounts. Only six in total said they made use of "section 11" funds (Local Government Act 1996); two used City Challenge funds; six used the single regeneration budget; and two claimed other sources. The proportion of expenditure derived from the Housing Revenue Account varied from nil (53% of authorities) to 100 per cent, with one in five (22%) claiming that 80 per cent or more of their expenditure was financed from it (Table 7.1). Half of these provided advice from dedicated advice sections within housing departments. Half the authorities who answered said that the general account was the source of all their spending on housing advice, and a further three in ten said that at least 60 per cent of their expenditure was derived from that source (Table 7.2). Four authorities (three districts and one London Borough) said that no part of the expenditure was met from the general account.

Table 7.1 — Local authority funding for housing advice services from housing revenue account (percentages)

| | Type of Authority | | | | All Authorities |
| | London Boroughs | | Metropolitan Councils | District Councils | |
	Inner	Outer			
Sample number	7	10	7	23	47
	%	%	%	%	%
No funding from this source	71	60	43	48	53
1 to 19.99%	14	10	29	9	13
20 to 39.99%	0	10	0	9	6
40 to 59.99%	14	0	14	4	6
60 to 79.99%	0	0	0	0	0
80 to 99.99%	0	10	0	13	9
100%	0	10	14	17	13

Source: *Telephone survey*

Table 7.2 — Local authority funding for housing advice services from general account (percentages)

| | Type of Authority | | | | All Authorities |
| | London Boroughs | | Metropolitan Councils | District Councils | |
	Inner	Outer			
Sample number	5	11	6	20	42
	%	%	%	%	%
No funding from this source	0	9	0	15	10
1 to 19.99%	0	9	0	10	7
20 to 39.99%	0	0	0	5	2
40 to 59.99%	20	0	0	0	2
60 to 79.99%	0	0	17	10	7
80 to 99.99%	20	36	17	15	21
100%	60	46	67	45	50

Source: *Telephone survey*

7.8   It seems unlikely to be appropriate that a high level of expenditure should be derived from the Housing Revenue Account, which is maintained in relation to the council's role as landlord, given the emphasis on other tenures and client groups in the work of advice services. Many housing officers were unable to say what was the source of revenue.

7.9   In the case studies local authorities expressed anxiety about the prospects of maintaining, let alone increasing, present levels of spending on housing advice services. They were being asked each year to find savings, and some saw a tension between maintaining existing staff levels, and funding the voluntary sector. In this context it might be expected that authorities would have sought to demonstrate value for money for housing advice services, but fewer than two in ten could identify savings in emergency accommodation as a result of housing advice. The sums saved varied from £5,500 to over

£2 million. One London borough calculated that the service paid for itself since the amount saved was almost exactly the same as the amount spent on the advice service in 1994/95. Of the nine authorities which could specify savings, four were London boroughs and four were districts; and five ran their service from a dedicated housing advice section. It is likely that having a separate section assists in the identification of costs, and the location in the housing department beside or near to homelessness staff assists in identifying savings on emergency accommodation.

Voluntary organisations' sources of funding

7.10   Many of the voluntary sector agencies which provide housing advice services are not set up - or funded - primarily to do so. Their role may be a more general advice role, or a specialist advice role - in which the provision of housing advice, or legal advice on housing, for example, may be expected by the funder, even though it is not spelled out explicitly. Similarly, social welfare agencies may be funded for their holistic support or advocacy role, or a more specific housing service role, in which funders may see advice as a legitimate part of the agency's work. Three in ten voluntary organisations overall said they were specifically funded to provide housing advice services. As might be expected, all the housing aid centres responding said they were, while lower proportions of the other types of agency said so.

7.11   When asked more generally about their sources of funding, the dominance of local government as funder became apparent, with 85 per cent overall in receipt of a local authority grant. Charitable donations were next most frequently mentioned, with just over half of the voluntary organisations (52%) saying they received them. Over one in ten (14%) received funding from their parent organisation, nine per cent received Section 73 funding, and 14 per cent received other central government funding. Almost seven in ten of the other specialist advice centres (mainly law centres) (69%) received legal aid fees, as did 24 per cent of the housing aid centres (Table 7.3).

7.12   In a two-tier local government system, housing authorities are the dominant sources of local authority funding. Seven voluntary organisations reported funding from county councils - not necessarily specifically for housing advice. One housing aid centre reported county council funding.

7.13   Only around one quarter of the local authorities (24%) were able to say how much they gave in grants to voluntary organisations for housing advice. The total amount varied from nil to over £807,000. Nine per cent of authorities identified grants of less than £19,999, and six per cent gave between £200,000 and £300,000. The majority of district councils who provided information on grants reported grants of less than £20,000, whereas the majority of London boroughs providing information gave more than £100,000.

7.14   It is likely that these figures understate the level of assistance to the voluntary sector from local government. For example, in some telephone interviews housing officers had no information on whether the authority provided financial assistance to the local CABx. It is also likely that some social welfare organisations, working with particular client groups, will receive funding from the social services authority. Housing authorities knew very little about such funding, which was found in case studies to take place through departments other than housing.

7.15   In the case studies, voluntary organisations were nearly all concerned about the implications of the financial climate for maintaining or extending their work. Some reported that the local authority which provided a grant was able to fund at the same cash level as before, or at a reduced level. For example, one CAB had reduced its spending to enable it to match its income, by reducing the paid working hours of the CAB manager, but she did not actually work a shorter week. In the survey, almost six in ten voluntary organisations (59%) said they had funding problems endangering their housing advice work in the previous 12 months. A larger proportion - eight in ten - could foresee a funding problem in the near future.

Table 7.3	Sources of funding for voluntary organisations 1994-95 (percentages)				
	Housing Advice	Other Specialist Advice	Generalist Advice	Social Welfare Agencies	All
Sample number	17	13	62	38	130
	%	%	%	%	%
Local authority grants	71	94	85	76	85
Donations	53	58	15	53	52
Parent organisations	18	15	0	16	14
Other central government	6	3	15	34	14
Legal aid funds	24	5	69	0	12
Fees	12	7	15	16	11
Section 73	29	0	0	16	9
Local authority contracts	0	10	0	10	8

Source: *Postal survey*

Local authority spending

7.16   Although only just over one third of authorities (36%) could identify any costs, this rose to 48 per cent for London boroughs, and 50 per cent for authorities with separate advice sections within their housing departments. However, the costs quoted did not always have a common basis. Some authorities found it difficult to identify non-staff expenses such as office and central administrative costs. The figures, therefore, have to be treated with caution. Just over half the authorities (55%) providing costs said they spent less than £200,000 per year, but nine per cent spent more than £500,000. The totals varied from £5,000 to over £1,048,000. In addition, two authorities reported expenditure of over one million pounds, possibly because they included the costs of neighbourhood offices which served a number of housing management functions. The majority of London boroughs and metropolitan authorities had costs of more than £200,000, while the majority of district councils identified costs of less than £20,000.

7.17   Staff costs generally accounted for the majority of costs, and varied from nil to £750,000. Over seven in ten authorities (72%) could not identify staff costs, but almost half the London boroughs could. Grants to voluntary organisations may be the second greatest call on local authority funds for housing advice, but few authorities were able to quantify them at all, and those who provided some information were often unable to say how much was given to CABx and social welfare organisations with a housing advice role. Of those able to provide any information, three in ten authorities (31%) reported spending more than £200,000 in 1994/95 on grants to voluntary organisations, and just over one third (35%) spent less than £20,000.

7.18   Only one authority and seven voluntary organisations reported that they had entered into contracts for the delivery of housing advice services (and a small number of other authorities were considering this approach).

7.19   Fewer than one third of the councils could identify staff training costs, and these varied from less than £500 in two district councils to more than £50,000 in one metropolitan authority. Over three quarters of those who supplied costs spent between £1000 and £10,000.

Voluntary organisation spending

7.20   A higher proportion of voluntary organisations than local authorities (66%) could say what they spent on providing services: spending varied from less than £25,000 in nine per cent to more than half a million pounds in four per cent of voluntary organisations. This spending was on all services, which in some cases included other forms of advice provision, and housing or welfare related services (Table 7.4). When asked how much was spent on housing advice services in 1994/5, a scant one third (32%) could say. However, all but one housing aid centre was able to say.

Table 7.4	Costs of voluntary organisations (all services) in 1994-95 (percentages)				
	Housing Advice	Generalist Advice	Specialist Advice	Social Welfare Agencies	All
Sample number	15	50	8	25	98
	%	%	%	%	%
Up to £24,999	20	8	0	8	9
£25,000 to 49,999	7	36	0	12	22
£50,000 to 74,999	7	12	13	8	10
£75,000 to 99,999	20	18	0	12	15
£100,000 to 199,999	27	20	50	28	26
£200,000 to 499,999	13	6	38	20	13
£500,000 or more	7	0	0	12	4

Source: *Postal survey*

7.21   Finally, almost half (47%) were able to say how much they spend on staff training and development for housing advice. In four per cent of cases the answer was nothing, and for nine per cent more it was less than £150. Just over half of those able to say, spent less than £1,000. Four per cent, including one housing aid centre, spent over £5,000.

Staff

7.22   Staffing resources are the most valuable asset an advice service has. Without staff, an advice agency is, at best, a library of books and leaflets which cannot convey the local knowledge, experience, expertise and empathy that advisers bring - leaving aside literacy issues. It is, therefore, appropriate that staffing costs should consume the greatest part of advice agencies' budgets.

Table 7.5	Local authorities and staff employed on housing advice				
	Percentage of Local Authorities with Staff				
	Service Type				All
Number of (FTE) Staff Employed	Separate Centre	Advice Section	Advice Staff	Part of Staff Duties	
Sample number	11	27	9	16	63
	%	%	%	%	%
Up to 2	0	0	22	6	5
From 2 up to 6	18	30	22	44	29
From 6 up to 10	18	22	33	6	19
From 10 up to 20	27	33	11	38	29
From 20 up to 30	27	7	0	0	8
From 30 up to 40	0	4	0	0	2
More than 40	9	4	11	6	6

Source: *Telephone survey*

7.23 In local authority housing advice services the number of staff (full time equivalent) was reported as being from one to 55.5 (Table 7.5). Only six per cent of councils reported more than 30, and two of these authorities were reporting staff with wider duties as being advice staff. Advice centres separate from housing departments employed fewer than 30 staff, with one exception. The separate housing advice sections created by many authorities employed from two to over forty staff. However, the average was between six and ten (Table 7.5).

7.24 As might be expected the majority of the voluntary organisations surveyed use at least some volunteers to provide the service. Over seven in ten (72%) were staffed by a mixture of paid and volunteer staff, almost one quarter (24%) only had paid staff, and three per cent had no paid staff. Almost two fifths (38%) of organisations surveyed said that the work done by paid and volunteer staff was the same (Table 7.6). Case study interviews suggest a number of ways in which work may differ: paid staff only may be involved in management tasks; paid staff may do follow up case work following a surgery conducted on a rota basis by a group of volunteers; volunteer staff may be involved in administration while paid staff are working with clients; paid staff may take more complex cases than volunteer staff; and volunteer staff may not do the more intensive counselling, mediation, or advocacy work.

Table 7.6	Staffing of voluntary organisations (percentages)				
	Housing Advice	Generalist Advice	Specialist Advice	Social Welfare Agencies	All
Sample number	18	66	17	47	148
	%	%	%	%	%
All paid staff	39	0	35	49	24
All volunteer staff	6	6	0	0	3
Mixture of paid and volunteer staff	56	94	65	51	72
Work done by volunteers is the same as that done by paid staff	38	32	53	40	38

Source: *Postal survey*

7.25 In voluntary organisations, the co-existence of paid and volunteer staff in many organisations is seen as a strength by the organisations themselves and by funders who may achieve remarkable value for money, for example, in their grant to enable a paid manager to co-ordinate the contributions of many volunteers. The possible nature of that "leverage" is shown in Table 7.7. For voluntary organisations with both paid and volunteer staff, the mean number of paid staff was 5.8 (full-time equivalent), and the mean number of volunteers was 5.2 (full-time equivalent). The mean number of paid staff is greater than the mean number of volunteers for all types of agency except the generalist advice agencies, where it is smaller, with 3.7 paid staff (FTE) and 10.7 volunteers (FTE). Most of these are CABx. This result demonstrates the huge contribution made to the work of generalist advice agencies by volunteers, and it demonstrates the risk taken to the work of a CAB, for example, if its grant suffers a small cut. This has a disproportionate effect on the resources of the bureau, and can lead, for example to managers or assistant managers reducing the hours they work (or are paid to work) in order to make the necessary savings.

7.26 In the case studies it was apparent that some voluntary sector advice agencies benefit from the expertise their volunteers bring through previous or present employment or training. For example, housing professionals may volunteer to help at a monthly evening surgery run by a housing aid centre; unemployed law graduates may work a few days a week in the local CAB; and women with professional social work or counselling qualifications may combine domestic responsibilities with work two mornings a week in a day centre. Volunteers with relevant jobs in housing and social services may receive training at their employer's expense which enhances their ability as a volunteer adviser. These volunteers bring staffing resources that are very welcome, but they also bring training and induction requirements - even when the volunteer has a professional qualification, he or she will need training, at the least, in the advice agency's procedures. A rapid turnover of volunteers can therefore pose a significant challenge for the paid or more permanent staff of an advice agency, or an agency that gives advice.

Table 7.7	Staffing levels of voluntary organisations (percentages)				
	Mean number of Staff (FTE)				
	Housing Advice	Generalist Advice	Specialist Advice	Social Welfare Agencies	All
Sample number	9	48	7	11	75
	%	%	%	%	%
Paid staff	5.35	3.96	5.50	4.45	4.40
Volunteer staff	1.51	7.83	4.29	3.41	6.16
All staff	7.28	11.71	9.29	7.77	10.37

Source: *Postal survey*

Staff training and development

7.27 Given the importance of staff in providing advice services it was important to establish whether they were given opportunities for training and development to ensure they were up to date, well-informed and skilled in their work.

7.28 Most local authorities said their staff had opportunities to take part in six different forms of training. All local authorities said they provided external short courses, and almost all (97%) said they were able to attend internal courses and seminars. Over nine in ten authorities said they provided on the job training. Almost as many (86%) offer a training element in team meetings. Two thirds (67%) provide opportunities for attending external qualifying courses. And almost six out of ten (57%) set time aside on a regular basis, although fewer than half (46%) of the district councils did so, compared with three quarters of the London boroughs. Overall this represents a considerable commitment to staff training and development, but it does not guarantee that all staff attend or that the content of the training is appropriate.

7.29 Local authorities were, therefore, asked about the training they provided in various advice related skills and in a number of housing topics. Around half (49 to 56%) of those who could answer provided training in interviewing, telephone advice work, mediation, counselling, advocacy, and debt counselling. Substantial minorities who provide mediation, counselling and advocacy services did not provide training in the skills required, although it is possible that skilled professionals or agencies were contracted or available to provide these services. Higher proportions of authorities said they provided training in housing-related topics - changes in homelessness and allocations policies; legal processes in housing; changes in the law on homelessness; changes in welfare benefits; and the implications of non-housing legislation such as community care or children-related legislation. At least nine in ten authorities provide training in all of these.

7.30 These results are hard to interpret. It may be that staff are already skilled in advice work and require updating in housing law and policy developments. The case studies suggest that authorities with case-work type services try to strike a balance in the training provided between advice skills and housing related training, and in other authorities, as might be expected, housing related training dominates.

7.31   For voluntary organisations there are some additional issues to consider about the skills of volunteers as well as paid staff. As has been shown, volunteers may be as qualified as paid staff, but questions may arise about whether they are kept up to date with new developments and skills. Almost eight in ten (79%) of the voluntary organisations surveyed said that they had a training budget for the year 1994/95, but fewer (59%) had a training strategy covering this period. The generalist advice agencies (many of which are CABx) did not reflect this general pattern: four in five (79%) had a training strategy, but slightly fewer (72%) had a training budget. This may, perhaps, be explained by CABx use of internal training, and NACAB and Shelter training on housing issues which is free to them under the NHAS scheme.

7.32   A substantial majority offered the same training to volunteer and paid staff (Table 7.8). More than eight in ten (83%) offered the same training on housing topics (such as homelessness legislation, and local authority policy) and the same skills training (for example, interviewing skills or debt counselling skills) to paid and unpaid staff.

Table 7.8	Staff training in voluntary organisations (percentages)				
	Housing Advice	Specialist Advice	Generalist Advice	Social Welfare Agencies	All
Sample number	12	15	57	42	126
	%	%	%	%	%
Training on housing topics is the same for paid and volunteer staff	75	80	93	74	83
Training on skills is the same for paid and volunteer staff	75	73	89	81	83
Have training budget	83	73	72	90	79
Have training strategy	50	20	79	48	59

Source: *Postal survey*

7.33   The most commonly available type of training for staff of voluntary organisations was external short courses, and over nine in ten (94%) made it available. More than eight in ten agencies (83%) also offered internal courses and seminars, and almost as many (80% respectively) had team meetings with a training element, and on the job coaching by senior staff. Just over half (54%) had a regular time set aside for training. Fewer than four in ten (39%) said that their staff could attend external qualifying courses by day release, block release, or evening study.

7.34   In general, higher proportions of staff in voluntary organisations than in local authorities are offered training in advice skills. Nine in ten agencies said they provided training in interviewing skills, and almost three quarters (74% respectively) provided training in telephone advice and advocacy skills. Two thirds (65 and 66% respectively) provide training in debt counselling and counselling. And over half (52%) provide it in mediation skills. Housing aid centres provide training particularly in telephone advice work, interviewing and advocacy.

7.35   Voluntary organisations also provide training in housing related topics. Almost all voluntary organisations surveyed (95%) offered training on changes to welfare benefits, and almost nine in ten provide it in the implications of non-housing legislation, changes in the law on homelessness, and changes in the law on housing. Over eight in ten (84% and 83% respectively) provide training in legal processes in housing, and in changes in local authority policies on homelessness and allocations.

7.36   These results show some differences between local authorities and voluntary organisations in the scope and extent of training. They lend support to the view that voluntary organisations are oriented more than local authorities to intensive case work, and that they have a firmer commitment to training in the advice skills which that implies. In the case studies it was found that training sometimes took place with workers from both sectors participating together, for example, a welfare benefits advice service provides training for housing, health, social work services and voluntary sector advice staff at the same time on changes in welfare benefits. There is scope for more training of that type, which would perhaps require some agencies to devote some resources to training, rather than to advice work

Summary

7.37   This chapter has reviewed the funding and staffing of housing advice services in the local authority and voluntary sectors. The results suggest that most local authorities need to develop a clearer focus on housing advice as a service area, as a step towards demonstrating value for money. Even in some of the dedicated advice services, senior staff were unsure of the costs of services, and had no model for calculating those benefits which can be quantified.

7.38   As far as could be established, the main source of funds for local authority advice services is the council's general account. Some authorities claim a contribution from the housing revenue account, but this would only be justified in as far as the advice service is for existing council tenants. Most voluntary organisations receive grants from local authorities, but for many this is one amongst a number of sources of income, suggesting that for many local authorities funding voluntary organisations may represent good value for money, but few authorities can demonstrate this. However, for some voluntary organisations, the reliance on a local authority grant combined with the use of volunteers makes them very vulnerable in the current public spending climate.

7.39   Both sectors demonstrate a strong commitment to the training and development of staff, including volunteers, but local authorities are less likely to train staff in advice skills which are relevant to the more intensive forms of advice work which characterise the work of many voluntary organisations.

8 Monitoring, Evaluation, and Quality

8.1   The growth of performance review in the public sector in the last 15 years has also affected voluntary organisations, which may wish to review or assess their effectiveness, as well as be required to demonstrate value for money by their funders. Systems for monitoring and evaluating performance against objectives have become well established in both sectors, although these developments have sometimes been criticised as unable to take account of the complex purposes of social services.

8.2   This chapter considers how far housing advice services have been affected by these trends. It considers the monitoring and evaluation systems in place within housing advice services, and the extent to which monitoring has been used as part of an evaluation or quality control system. Some examples of systems in use, or which are being developed are described, and some of the problems and issues that emerge in practice are considered.

Monitoring
Purpose of monitoring

8.3   Organisations need to know what they are doing and whether they are achieving the objectives they set for themselves or which others set for them. They, therefore, need to design monitoring systems which capture the information that will enable them to answer the questions they or others such as their clients or their funders may have about what they do. Monitoring has to be planned, systematic, and linked with a process of review or evaluation which makes sense of the monitoring information and reaches judgements about how well an organisation is performing. Organisations need to have a clear idea why they are collecting the data and the use that will be made of it.

8.4   Given the multiple objectives held by some advice services, and the uncertainty of others about what their objectives are (see Chapter 3), it is not surprising that monitoring and evaluation systems were not well developed in some advice services. In contrast, a few in both the voluntary and statutory sectors had sophisticated systems introduced for a variety of reasons, such as to demonstrate effectiveness to funders, to assess value for money for the organisation itself, or to meet some standard of performance set down for management or validation purposes.

Information needs

8.5   Advice agencies should be assisted in their monitoring by the fact that providing housing advice requires information about clients to be collected so that, for example, the case-worker can hold relevant information about the details of the client's case. However, information required for the provision of a service is not necessarily the right information required for monitoring or auditing purposes.

8.6   Virtually all providers of housing advice, from local authority advice centres to small community groups or accommodation providers, collect information about their work in some way. But there is no uniformity between these different types of agencies in how the information is collected or used; whether it is used in any systematic way for review purposes; in what is monitored; in how complex enquiries are categorised; or in the use made of the resulting data. To some extent this reflects the intrinsic difficulties of measuring advice and its outcomes, as many of the housing advice centre managers in the local authority and voluntary sectors are aware.

8.7   The variation is illustrated by the ways in which agencies collect information about numbers of clients and cases, as Chapter 5 showed. Beyond this there are differences in the details of personal characteristics collected, and difficulties in monitoring outcomes, although most agencies try to do so. There are three distinct categories of information commonly collected by agencies in both sectors:

- client characteristics;

- type of problem(s);

- outcomes of advice.

In addition, a growing number of agencies seek to measure client satisfaction.

Local authorities

8.8   Almost three quarters (73%) of local authorities record the characteristics of their clients, although some made the point that only clients who are accepted as "cases" were monitored in this way. Casual enquiries and telephone contact is often not monitored. At its simplest, the numbers of enquiries by people with different characteristics provide a rough picture of the changing demand for a service over time; but the fact that agencies use different systems for collecting information makes for difficulties in comparing patterns.

8.9   District authorities are less likely to record client characteristics than London and metropolitan authorities, with fewer than two thirds (64%) saying they do so, compared with almost nine in ten London boroughs (86%) and almost as high a proportion of metropolitan authorities (82%). The nature and organisation of the advice service may have been the key factor: authorities with advice centres separate from the housing department, or housing advice sections within their housing departments, were most likely to monitor characteristics (83% and 79% respectively). Least likely were authorities where housing advice is available only as part of the homelessness duty (66%) (Table 8.1).

8.10   Almost nine out of ten of those who monitor characteristics record the tenure of the client (88%), and the age of the client (86%). Three quarters (74%) record ethnic origin, and slightly more record age (78%) and details of dependants (81%). Around half record income (45%), social security benefits received (53%) and employment status (59%). Other characteristics mentioned included pregnancy and the baby's estimated date of birth, local connection, disabilities and health problems, and any care history.

8.11   Monitoring the reasons why people seek housing advice is a way of identifying local trends in housing problems. Overall, seven out of ten authorities (69%) said that they recorded the nature of the housing enquiry or problem in a standardised way (Table 8.1). District authorities were least likely to monitor the nature of the problem (59%) than London and metropolitan authorities (both 82%). As might be expected, where an authority has a separate advice centre, or advice section within the housing department, they are more likely to monitor the nature of the problem (respectively 83% and 82% do). Barely half (49%) of the authorities who provide advice only as part of their homelessness duties recorded the nature of the problem.

8.12   Almost two thirds (63%) of authorities attempt to record the outcome of the advice given to clients. This can be difficult if clients lose touch and do not inform their housing adviser what has happened to them. Just over half (54%) of district councils recorded outcomes, whereas over two thirds of other types of authority did so. Over seven out of ten authorities with separate advice centres and separate housing advice sections recorded outcomes. Successful outcomes such as rehousing were attributed to the advice provided, and were used in a few cases to demonstrate value for money for the advice service.

8.13   Seeking feedback from clients about their views on the service provided has become a well-established method of monitoring in some public services. Overall, fewer than four in ten authorities (37%) did this in relation to housing advice services. The methods used ranged from contracting independent researchers to conduct focus groups and individual interviews with a range of clients, to a complaints system prominently advertised. However, authorities with different types of advice services varied greatly in the extent to which they sought client feedback. Three quarters (75%) of the authorities with advice centres separate from their housing departments did so, compared with just over four in ten of the authorities (43%) with housing advice sections and fewer than one in five (18%) of authorities with no advice service extending beyond their homelessness advice and assistance duties.

8.14   The most common method of seeking feedback was a sample survey of clients. One authority carries out such a survey of all clients visiting the council's housing advice centre during one week every two months, an unusually short internal between surveys. Another authority conducted what is intended to become an annual survey of all first time callers to its HAC over a one month period, using a simple questionnaire. Questions concentrated on the accessibility of the service in terms of finding and travelling to the premises and the suitability of appointment time offered, the quality of the service, how useful the advice was, how clearly the advice was explained, and the time given by the adviser. As a result of this feedback the HAC has begun allocating longer appointment times.

Table 8.1	Local authorities and monitoring and evaluation records (percentages)					
Monitoring Information Collected	Separate Centre	Separate Section	Separate Staff	Part of Staff Duties	No Separate Service	All
Sample number	12	28	10	20	33	103
	%	%	%	%	%	%
Client characteristics	83	79	70	70	66	73
Nature of enquiry	83	82	70	75	49	69
Outcome	75	71	50	60	58	63
Client feedback	75	43	40	35	18	37

Source: *Telephone survey*

Voluntary organisations

8.15   Monitoring in the voluntary sector may be designed and implemented by an agency for its own purposes, or, increasingly commonly, organisations may be required to produce evidence of the quality and quantity of their work by funding bodies. Monitoring can be used for very different purposes, such as to inform campaigning, or to provide information on the quantity, nature or quality of the advice service itself. Some voluntary organisations had systems of monitoring and evaluation in place long before value for money scrutinies became a feature of the public sector. NACAB, for example, has for many years reviewed individual CABx against criteria for membership of the association, which relate to issues such as training, use of the NACAB information system, and equal opportunities.

8.16   Individual CABx record: client characteristics (gender, ethnicity, age group); method of contact; whether enquirers are new or repeat callers; case category, in which housing is part of a wider category "housing, property, and land", one of eight categories; phone calls, letters written, or referrals made on behalf of the client; and time taken. CAB managers in case studies emphasised that while they recognise a need for monitoring, the time taken to fully record these details can be seen as over long by advisers, who are often under pressure.

8.17   Several housing aid centres use a system called CRESS for recording details of clients and their problems, and for monitoring. The system was initially developed for Shelter and has since been adapted for use by other agencies. It provides basic information in tabular form monthly or at other intervals, and it allows an agency more easily to monitor some aspects of what it is doing than a manual system would. It is not an evaluation system, but could play a part in one. Some interviewees suggested that a more flexible and easy to use system could be developed using more up to date computers and software, but the resources to develop a new system are not available.

8.18   Around two thirds or more voluntary organisations were found to collect information about four basic aspects of their service: the characteristics of clients; the nature of the enquiry or problem; the outcome of the case; and the views of clients on the service or advice provided (Table 8.2). Eight in ten (80%) record the nature of the client's problem, and almost as many (73%) record the housing outcome. Around two thirds (67% and 66% respectively) record the characteristics of the client and seek feedback on their clients' views about the service. The most favoured method for client feedback is the sample survey, which almost six out of ten (57%) of those who seek feedback use.

Table 8.2	Voluntary organisations and monitoring and evaluation records (percentages)				
Monitoring Information Collected	Housing Advice	Other Specialist Advice	General Advice	Social Welfare Agencies	All
Sample number	12	47	11	41	137
	%	%	%	%	%
Client characteristics	100	50	80	76	67
Nature of enquiry	88	86	87	63	80
Outcome	94	67	80	73	73
Client feedback	59	70	53	66	66

Source: *Postal survey*

8.19   *Housing Information and Advice: A Base Line Study*[1] reports on a survey of user satisfaction with housing advice and information providers across Scotland. The handling of enquirers is found to be the key to providing satisfaction: "Ease of contact by telephone or in person, knowledgeable staff who are able to deal with the problem and tell enquirers everything they want to know, in private, and the provision of written information all tend to produce very satisfied customers."[2] These issues are all measurable, and related directly to the clients' views of the service provided, while other attempts to monitor user satisfaction have focused on the outcomes of advice.

8.20   For local authorities and voluntary sector housing aid centres the characteristics most commonly monitored are those most relevant to housing need. Commitment to equal opportunities strategies would suggest a need to monitor characteristics such as ethnic origin, with a view to ensuring that the service is reaching all sections of the community, and in particular those groups who are most likely to face housing difficulty through poverty or discrimination. Yet almost one half of local authorities (46%) do not record ethnic origin. Use of postcode monitoring would allow the mapping of patterns by area, but no such systematic use of postcodes was encountered. Figure 8.1 sets out the types of monitoring encountered in the surveys and case studies and reports the sorts of reasons cited by interviewees about why the information was collected, as well as the problems encountered.

1.   Gibson, P. & Johnston, L. (1995) *Housing Information and Advice: A Baseline Study and Evaluation Framework on Use of Services*, Edinburgh: Homepoint, Scottish Homes, p.56.
2.   Chariton (1995) *Housing Information and Advice Services National Standards and Good Practice Manual*, Edinburgh: Homepoint, Scottish Homes.

8.21   The data collected from clients may be limited by issues of sensitivity and confidentiality. To clarify the causes of homelessness and the problems associated with it, agencies may seek to maximise the information recorded, including information about sensitive issues such as sexuality, mental health, care histories, and prior abuse. Clients may not want this information to be recorded for a variety of reasons, and this could lead to a potential conflict between the wishes of the client and the requirements of funding and accountability systems which tend to stress the need for recording.

8.22   In interviews a number of housing advisers, and people working with homeless people on the streets, discussed the reluctance of some of their clients to answer personal questions which they see as being unnecessarily intrusive and as having no relevance to the problems which they face. For example, a worker at one day centre found it impossible to monitor sexuality (although it was seen as desirable to do so) because many of her clients perceived the question to be asking about HIV status. Similarly, telephone clients may be unwilling to answer monitoring questions about issues such as age and ethnic origin. Clients who are paying for the phone call are said to resent the time taken by monitoring questions: many clients of housing advice services will be poor or in debt.

8.23   Sensitive information needs to be stored safely, and access to it limited. One voluntary organisation was unable to complete our survey due to a recent burglary in which the computer on which the data was stored had been stolen, and cabinets containing casework information were ransacked.

Evaluation
Using monitoring data

8.24   Monitoring by advice organisations, if thorough and well designed, should reveal who is served, what their problems are, the advice that is given to them, and whether they overcome their problems. Potentially this is very rich data that could assist in mapping the demand for advice of different sorts, and should assist in evaluating the costs and benefits of advice services.

8.25   Agencies varied in their use of the data collected. At one end of a spectrum were local authorities and voluntary organisations with sophisticated monitoring systems geared either alone, or simultaneously, to purposes of management control, or quality assessment, or to supporting staff. Staff had targets to meet, supervisors inspected case-notes, and performance reports were prepared regularly for committees. Case studies suggested that the use of casework monitoring and file reviews by senior staff as a means of checking the quality of advice offered is particularly common in local authorities with dedicated advice centres and sections. A sample of cases might be reviewed every month or every three months, for example. This might or might not be complemented with meetings between case-workers and their supervisor which would allow either party to raise any issues arising in the case-work or the job more generally.

8.26   Voluntary organisations with such methods included those taking part in the Legal Aid Board's non-solicitor advice agency pilot which involved external auditors reviewing case records. However, often these agencies previously had a system for monitoring and review in place involving senior staff. In addition, management committees may have a role in evaluating performance, especially of senior staff.

8.27   Authorities with dedicated advice sections within their housing departments were most likely to produce regular reports, with almost nine in ten (89%) doing so. These reports typically extend to several pages, containing a lot of statistics. They are produced for housing or other committees, or they may be made more widely available, in which case they often serve a dual purpose by also providing publicity for the service. It is common for these reports to illustrate the work that the advisers are involved in through case studies of recent cases.

8.28   At the other end of the spectrum were organisations which collated minimal information, and did not use it to assess performance. In local authorities, the information required for the returns on homelessness to the Department of the Environment were typically seen as sufficient. Although three quarters of authorities overall (75%) said they produced monitoring or evaluation reports at regular intervals, almost one half of this number, 32 per cent of all authorities, said that they produced only reports in relation to the advice duties under the homelessness legislation. An example of this sort of report is a rural district authority which produces a one page sheet every three months, showing the number of homelessness enquiries received, the number requiring investigation, and the number of enquirers given advice and assistance only.

8.29 Collection of data did not guarantee that use would be made of it. Staff in both sectors reported having difficulty in devoting time to analysis and evaluation, and in the voluntary sector this was more likely to be compounded by lack of computer technology.

Achieving objectives in the local authority sector

8.30 Virtually all local authorities (98%) identified the prevention or alleviation of homelessness as an *objective* in the provision of housing advice (see Table 3.1). Yet when asked what method was used for measuring the contribution of advice to the prevention of homelessness, over seven in ten of authorities (71%) were unable to identify any particular method. The London Boroughs are most likely to measure the contribution of advice to the prevention of homelessness, with almost two thirds (64%) using a specific method, whereas fewer than one in five (18%) of district authorities use an identified method (Table 8.3).

Figure 8.1	Topics commonly monitored by local authorities and voluntary organisations		
Categories of Monitoring	**Examples**	**Reasons for Monitoring**	**Problems in Monitoring**
Client characteristics	race; age; gender; tenure, if any; alcohol / drug use; area they live in; employment status; household type;	to ensure that service is reaching all sections of population; to establish patterns of need in different population groups; to help ensure that services are culturally appropriate	may be sensitive for client; client may see as irrelevant; may be especially difficult in the case of outreach / streetwork, or telephone advice; need to guard against infringing confidentiality
Type of problem	mortgage repossession; harassment; rent arrears; homelessness; rooflessness; need for disability aids / adaptations	to encourage policy development on particular areas; local and national campaigning; to inform training strategy; to ensure advice services well targeted on need	difficulties in consistent categorising; problems are often multi faceted
Success of advice	homelessness prevented; successfully rehoused; landlord prosecuted; benefits claimed; repairs achieved	fund-raising; to encourage others to use the service (by portraying it as successful); to check on the quality of advice	at what stage is the outcome measured; agencies often do not know what the outcome was; outcome may be unrelated to the advice given (advice may not have been followed / problem may have been unresolvable)
Other	client satisfaction; referring agency; action taken by adviser; adviser caseload; waiting times for appointments; casual enquiries / telephone queries / casework; costs saved	service review; monitor demand; demonstrate value for money	satisfaction may be linked with outcomes, not advice given; costs saved are hard to measure

8.31   Authorities with no advice service beyond their homelessness duty are least likely (92%) to measure the contribution of advice to the prevention of homelessness. These authorities restrict their advice role largely to non-priority cases, and so the cost of any homelessness arising will not fall directly on the authority's housing budgets, which may explain the lack of measurement. Measuring the contribution of advice is most commonly done (by 16% of authorities) by measuring savings on emergency accommodation. Only two authorities attempted to measure the length of occupancy secured.

Table 8.3	Local authorities and measuring the contribution of advice to the prevention of homelessness (percentages)			
	Type of Authority			All Authorities
	London Boroughs	Metropolitan Councils	District Councils	
Sample number	22	22	61	105
	%	%	%	%
No method	36	73	82	71
Savings on emergency accommodation	36	5	13	16
Length of occupancy secured	5	0	2	2
Other	23	18	3	11

Source: *Telephone survey*

8.32   Authorities were able to suggest a number of additional formal and less formal ways of judging performance that were used within their authorities:

- number of clients who have heard about the service through past users;

- targets regarding time taken to see people, punctuality for appointments, closing cases, and responding to telephone calls and letters;

- avoiding judicial review;

- numbers rehoused;

- levels of benefits achieved for clients;

- level of use of the complaints procedure;

- the number of landlords prosecuted (although it was not stated whether success meant more prosecutions or fewer).

8.33   The overall impression gained is one of huge variety in the extent and nature of quality assessment. Two factors seemed most important in an authority having any systematic approach: first, authorities with the most developed advice services were most likely to have attempted to assess the value for money and effectiveness of these services; and secondly, from the case studies, authorities with the most developed techniques were likely also to have applied them generally throughout the authority. Their practice may have been driven by enthusiasm for performance review in general, rather than specifically for its use in housing or housing advice services.

Achieving objectives in the voluntary sector

8.34   Voluntary sector advice agencies in case studies were more likely than local authorities to be able to point to a system of management or quality control which was intended to provide reassurances about effectiveness or value for money. The emphasis, however, as in local authorities, is more on measuring inputs than outcomes. Social welfare organisations which provide housing advice amongst other services were equally concerned about quality, but understandably, their systems were not necessarily geared to isolate the housing advice aspect of their work from other aspects.

8.35   Quality control in the voluntary sector advice field is developing for a number of reasons, including as a result of pressure on agencies to demonstrate value for money, and the development of legal aid funding for non-solicitor agencies. The systems outlined below vary in their origins and the extent to which they are imposed on organisations or developed by them in a more organic way. The following discussion is intended to provide a review of a varied and fast developing field.

Citizen's Advice Bureaux

8.36   Internal evaluation focuses on an annual quantification of the key problem areas presented by CAB clients, summarised in annual reports. This information is entered into a central information bank from which NACAB monitors changes in demand, and identifies social policy issues on which to campaign. NACAB insist on standard systems, as otherwise it would be impossible to compare data from different bureaux.

8.37   Quality assurance is carried out through three yearly reviews which focus on a set of criteria, including training, equal opportunities, and adherence to NACAB standards for information provision. In addition, development support is provided by NACAB regional offices. NACAB, therefore, has in place one of the most developed systems for delivering quality advice in the voluntary sector. The emphasis, though, is on inputs and procedures, rather than on measuring the quality of advice actually delivered. It is also limited in the extent to which it measures ease of access, such as getting through on the telephone.

NHAS

8.38   Monitoring of the NHAS scheme is determined by the demands of the Department of the Environment. Shelter submit records of the number of training events they run and advice staff attending, items of information issued to participating agencies, and the use of consultancy and referral services, compared against agreed targets. Information is given on the number of bureaux operating NHAS, their opening hours and staffing levels, the number of housing and homelessness related enquiries, and advice given or action taken.

HomePoint Standards Manual

8.39   HomePoint, the Housing Information and Advice project established by Scottish Homes to improve the overall provision of housing information and advice in Scotland, published a manual providing standards for the provision of housing advice services in 1995.[3] The standards specify how an agency should set about providing a housing advice service, and provide detailed checklists of the questions and issues that arise in dealing with particular enquiries. The emphasis is on procedures and inputs, rather than outcomes. The standards are not part of an accreditation system, so there are no sanctions available to impose them. They have been provided to encourage a voluntary approach to standards in the first instance, and an accreditation system may grow from their adoption by a wide range of organisations. The manual has been well received by a number of advice agencies.

Advice Services Alliance

8.40   The Advice Services Alliance is an association of the large federations of advice agencies, including NACAB and FIAC. The member networks vary in their monitoring systems and standardisation. As an umbrella for these groups ASA is concerned that standards are established, and is working towards agreed monitoring which would enable groups to compare like with like. The ASA has no power to lay down guidelines on monitoring or any other issue. The sensitivity of organisations about their own standards, and scarcity of resources, make it difficult for the ASA to develop standards, and member networks have their own different cultures. However ASA tries to encourage networks to learn from one another. In consultation with member bodies the ASA has produced a set of core standards intended not as a checklist, but as the basis on which criteria for service specification, policies and service reviews can be developed. As such, the standards remains general statements of intent: for example, the advice centre should have appropriate induction and on going training for staff, and there will be systematic procedures for monitoring the standards of service.

---

3.   Advice Services Alliance (undated) *The Case for Advice 2,000* (leaflet).

8.41   Representing both generalist agencies (NACAB, Citizens Advice Scotland, FIAC), specialist agencies (Shelter, Law Centres Federation), and client oriented groups (Youth Access, DIAL UK) ASA recognises that the different levels of provision require different standards. For example, standards designed for specialists in housing advice provision could not reasonably be expected from CABx. However certain criteria such as accessibility, complaints procedures, equal opportunities and insurance can be common to all.

CHAS

8.42   The CHAS groups' regular meetings were used as a forum in which to develop a standards manual for the use of the individual groups. A number of working parties involving committee members and paid staff were set up to examine different aspects of housing aid work. The manual was then drafted from the results of these deliberations and accepted by them all. The manual's contents are considered by some groups to have done no more than confirm the sort of good practice, in relation to equal opportunities policies, for example, which they already had in place. Other groups found it a useful process because it enabled them to address issues that had been neglected as their time and resources were devoted to the provision of advice. The manual is short, and considers issues such as staff and committee roles. The process of development seems to have achieved a sense of ownership amongst all the groups, which a more prescriptive process might not have achieved.

Legal Aid Franchising Scheme

8.43   The Legal Aid Board is experimenting with the extension of legal services into areas of social welfare law not well served at present, by allowing non-solicitor advice agencies to receive legal aid funds to provide services. So far, the scheme has involved a pilot experiment in which around 40 agencies, half of which are CABx, are paid a set fee for the provision of advice services in specific areas of law, of which housing is one. The scheme is being monitored by a research team. In parallel, the Board has introduced a scheme to ensure quality standards are maintained in law practices and centres that are franchised to provide legal aid funded advice. These standards are applied equally in the non-solicitor agencies. The pilot experiment was agreed in consultation with a number of representative advice alliances (including the ASA, FIAC, NACAB, and the Law Centres Federation).

8.44   There are two systems for monitoring quality in the franchise scheme.[4] First, applicants must meet the franchising specification which sets out standards in relation to the process of providing advice: client care, complaints systems, equal opportunities, and in relation to management issues such as recruitment and financial control. Second, the Board audits a sample of casework files regularly to assess the work of the franchisee against criteria which a competent practitioner would be expected to have covered. Further monitoring on case outcomes, client satisfaction, and the average costs of cases is expected to be developed further into the process. The impact on agencies of the monitoring process has in some cases been substantial:

> They have been required within a very short period to document, and in some cases develop from scratch, a comprehensive range of office and casework procedures. They face a level of continuous monitoring which is far more rigorous than that generally undertaken by funders. For the purposes of the research they are required to assess green form eligibility (for Legal Aid) and time record casework so that the researchers can calculate productivity and as far as possible make cost comparisons with solicitors.[5]

8.45   Several agencies encountered in the case studies were involved in the pilot schemes for extending legal aid to non-solicitor agencies. For example, the Legal Services Committee in Norwich (a voluntary organisation providing free legal advice and housing repossession support) has established entirely new office and supervision systems. This is seen as a positive outcome now that they are in place, but the time spent on preparing

---

4.   Jenner, R. (1995) 'Advice Agencies and Franchising' in *Advisor* (48), pp.6-8.
5.   Jenner, R. (1995) op. cit. p.7.

the franchise bid and meeting the specifications could have been spent fund-raising for other purposes or advising clients. CHAS Kirklees has also been able to appoint an additional adviser. The quality standards were not difficult to achieve - most of the necessary procedures were in place, though some changes to existing systems had to be made. The process of bidding was onerous, but the benefit is seen in additional resources to provide more advice, and in extending the aid centre's range of funders. Oldham CAB was also franchised to provide money and debt advice, which usually includes a housing dimension. The bureau finds it onerous to comply with some of the record keeping involved, such as noting a two minute phone call. However, this bureau also found it reasonably easy to cope with the work involved in making the bid, and sees the same advantages of increased resources for advice work as well as extending the range of funders. One potential disadvantage is that regular "support" meetings between advisers and managers could be in danger of becoming "supervision" only meetings, in order to ensure that the quality criteria are met, although in practice staff have achieved their targets.

Qualification for advice staff

8.46   There are no recognised professional qualifications in advice work, though advisers in voluntary organisations had a wide range of educational and professional backgrounds. Only solicitors, as professionals, come under the authority of the Law Society and its standards. Therefore, this, in theory, is external control, but in practice Law Centres tend to receive little attention from the Law Society.

8.47   National Vocational Qualifications are being developed for advice work. These would provide work-based and nationally recognised qualifications at different levels for staff and volunteers if they wished to gain a formal qualification. Level One is to be about advice provision generally, and there may in future be attempts to develop higher level qualifications in specialised advice work. This will have the effect of setting standards for advice staff. This is why ASA is supporting the development of NVQs, as they will establish a minimum level of competence.

Summary

8.48   This chapter has reviewed the monitoring information collected by advice agencies and the use they make of it for evaluation purposes. There is a strong interest in both the statutory and voluntary sectors to improve on present systems of monitoring and evaluation, with the aims of developing a more comprehensive framework. An evaluation framework capable of coping with the multiple objectives of advice work, and of adaptation to the different practices and cultures of different types of agency, was not apparent. Advice agencies in both sectors have developed some elements of such a framework and would benefit from collaborating to achieve more, as some are trying to do.

8.49   A varied pattern emerged in which local authorities with the most developed housing advice services were most likely to collect information and to use it to review performance. However, the data collected often reflected the information obtained in the course of delivering advice services, rather than the information required to make a systematic assessment of the achievement of objectives in advice provision. Local authorities often found it hard to devote sufficient time to using the data they collected for evaluation purposes. They were using a variety of systems and methods for monitoring, and would be likely to benefit from coming together to review methods for evaluation in a difficult and complex service area, in which most agencies have multiple objectives.

8.50   In the voluntary sector there was also variety between different types of agency, but within certain networks there were standard systems for monitoring and evaluation. However, as in the local authority sector, the data collected often reflected the information easily obtained about inputs rather than information required to make a systematic assessment of the achievement of their objectives in advice provision. Staff and volunteers often found it hard to devote sufficient time to using the data they collected for evaluation purposes, and resource and technology constraints were a particular impediment.

9 Models of Practice in Housing Advice Services

9.1   This chapter provides guidance about a range of options for the development of housing advice services. It considers the implications of the patterns of housing advice provision reported in previous chapters, and outlines alternative models for different aspects of housing advice provision. It is presented under a series of key headings which might form a checklist for those involved in developing local strategies for housing advice provision. The models identified are not necessarily encountered in practice, where mixed models are more likely to emerge, but they are presented because they help to identify the nature of the key options available to local authorities and other agencies in the development of housing advice services. The chapter does not, therefore, provide a prescription of action to be taken in particular localities since that will vary according to local circumstances, but it does provide guidance on the range of options available.

9.2   The key action points identified for local consideration are:

- set up a strategy making mechanism;

- audit provision within an agreed framework for audit and review of services;

- identify and clarify existing and future roles in the local authority and voluntary sectors;

- consider who is served, and needs unmet;

- assess networks;

- define and agree working arrangements;

- assess resources required and available from all sources;

- consider quality and evaluation issues;

- agree service developments;

- publicise availability of advice services.

A strategy making mechanism

9.3   Few local authorities have a strategy for the provision and development of housing advice services, but many felt they should, a view shared by the voluntary sector. This interest arises from a number of factors: concerns about funding levels and value for money in the local authority and voluntary sectors; the implications of a new statutory duty on local authorities to secure comprehensive advice services; the development of an "enabling" role to encompass advice on private sector housing options; and the desire to do more to assist homeless people and other vulnerable groups. Authorities and voluntary organisations recognise that a strategy could serve a number of purposes, but different agencies may have a commitment to developing a strategy for different reasons.

9.4   The purposes a local strategy might serve include:

- stating the authority's and others' objectives in housing advice provision;

- reviewing the existing level of provision;

- achieving some common understanding with other advice providers about roles and relationships;

- setting down a programme for service development over the medium term;

- reviewing funding and stating the authority's broad intentions for the future;

- agreeing policy areas for joint work, collaboration and service development with other agencies;

- setting up mechanisms for reviewing policies and services.

9.5   Someone needs to take the initiative locally in developing strategies. The local authority is likely to be seen as the agency with most independence and legitimacy in taking an overview, partly due to its strategic and funding roles, providing it conducts these with respect for the contribution other agencies are playing or could play. It also has a strategic role in relation to other types of advice, for which a policy framework may already be in place. In practice, though, another agency, such as an independent housing aid centre, or a federation of voluntary organisations, could take the initiative in relation to housing if it were seen as sufficiently legitimate.

9.6   The local authority strategic role could involve:

- researching locally the exact nature of provision and the roles of agencies;

- identifying needs, gaps and any overlaps in provision;

- funding provision by voluntary sector agencies;

- drawing up, preferably in collaboration with others, a development plan to monitor, evaluate and improve provision;

- facilitating the initiation or development of networks to enhance provision;

- co-ordinating the work of agencies in the public, private and voluntary sectors.

9.7   This is broadly the role seen for the lead agencies - mainly local authorities - in the Scottish Homes HomePoint local strategies project. The good practice guide arising from that project provides guidance for local authorities and other agencies on the development of local strategies.[1]

9.8   In practice there are many ways in which strategies can be developed and this study has not found evidence to support any particular single approach. The case studies demonstrated a variety of local contexts making some approaches more successful in some areas than others. Important factors, more apparent in some areas than others in practice, were:

- the collation of information about existing services, their purpose, client groups, and the nature and extent of use and needs;

- clarity about the role the local authority itself wishes to play, and the implications for the voluntary sector;

- development of liaison arrangements for strategic planning and service delivery;

- consideration of the roles of different agencies within the statutory, commercial and voluntary sectors;

- consideration of funding sources and needs;

- consideration of issues of quality and effectiveness of services.

9.9   In virtually all parts of the country, the expertise of some part of the major networks of housing advice providers (Shelter, CHAS, FIAC and CABx) as well as other local agencies, can contribute to the development of strategies. Other expertise is available

---

1. John Palmer and Peter Gibson (1996) *Local Housing Information and Advice Strategies: a good practice guide*, Homepoint.

amongst voluntary organisations who serve homeless and other disadvantaged people. In addition, local government departments apart from housing may have a role in advice provision, particularly for the most vulnerable. Clearly such agencies have a direct interest in the development of services, but authorities should be able to weigh that interest along with others in its decision making processes, and seek to work with the voluntary sector in the development of services.

Auditing provision

9.10   An audit of provision in the voluntary sector as well as within several local government departments, such as social services, is essential before any planning for service development can take place. Housing departments need to know about the number and nature of voluntary organisations and others providing advice, even when neither "housing" nor "advice" are their main function, and about their funding, including all contributions from the local authority.

9.11   This knowledge can be acquired by a variety of means, such as through an established forum, by carrying out a questionnaire survey backed up with visits and interviews (as conducted by some authorities), and requesting basic information such as that contained in the annual reports of CABx (see 8.36). Agencies will appreciate being asked directly about their work, and will then expect to be kept informed about how the information is used.

Agency purposes and roles

9.12   Within the statutory and voluntary sectors four broad objectives or purposes of housing advice have been detected (Chapter 3):

> achieving **citizenship** rights to information and advice
>
> illuminating **policy** impacts or weaknesses
>
> assisting the exercise of **rights** to decent housing
>
> assisting **market efficiency**.

9.13   It is helpful if local authorities and voluntary organisations can be clear about which of these they are attempting to meet. In addition, it is necessary to know how agencies interpret "advice", since the nature of the service provided is largely determined by the definition adopted. One account of the range of meanings is:

> straightforward information
>
> explanation
>
> advice such as setting out possible options
>
> practical aid such as helping with form filling
>
> referral to another source of help
>
> mediation
>
> counselling
>
> advocacy.[2]

9.14   Clarifying roles and purposes may reveal differences in the objectives of voluntary organisations and a local authority. Clarity about objectives is also essential in order to monitor and evaluate services. Voluntary organisations have autonomy to establish their own aims, and sometimes their work will conflict with the work and objectives of local authorities. However, many authorities will readily acknowledge that they alone would have difficulty in providing for the needs met by the voluntary sector. Authorities also value the resources voluntary organisations may bring to their work from volunteers, charitable donations, central government and the private sector.

---

2.   Scottish Homes (1992) *Housing Information And Advice: You Can't Ask A Leaflet Questions*, Scottish Homes.

9.15   Clarity about the variety of style, approach, role and purpose between agencies may reduce some of the tension which inevitably arises at local level given competition for limited resources, for example. A service audit can also identify whether there is wasteful overlap or useful additional provision. In principle, there is nothing wrong with a plurality or overlap of provision, providing objectives and roles have been clarified, and liaison arrangements are satisfactory. Indeed it would be impossible to standardise agency roles even if this were felt by some to be a good idea.

The voluntary sector

9.16   In the voluntary sector, broadly, two types of voluntary organisation can be distinguished: agencies whose explicit remit is to provide advice (called here *advice agencies*), and agencies which provide advice amongst other social welfare services (called *social welfare agencies*). Social welfare agencies may work intensively with disadvantaged groups such as young homeless people and may provide a more holistic advocacy and counselling service than a generalist agency or specialist housing aid centre can do. The nature of these roles is little researched. Social welfare agencies do not often describe their role as "advice" and infrequently identify housing advice as one of their roles, yet in practice this may be the case. These two types can be further categorised with reference to the subject matter they deal with. Some provide services across a variety of policy or service fields, others specialise in housing or other fields relevant to housing such as law, or community care. The typology of voluntary organisations which results from this categorisation is shown at Figure 9.1.

Figure 9.1	Types of voluntary organisation providing housing advice		
	Nature of Advice Role		
		Specialist	
Type of Agency	**Generalist**	**Housing**	**Other**
Advice Agencies	eg CAB	eg local Shelter HAC	eg law centre, disability advice service
Social Welfare organisations (whose work includes housing advice)	eg residents' associations	eg housing associations	eg Women's Aid, Age Concern

9.17   Private sector organisations, such as building societies and solicitors, are not the focus of this report, but the potential contribution of some of them to the alleviation of housing problems has been realised, particularly since the growth in the incidence of mortgage arrears in the early 1990s (see 3.30). Some initiatives in advice provision have therefore involved private sector agencies in funding, in collaboration with other agencies, and in the direct provision of advice.

Local housing authorities

9.18   Housing authorities can play broadly two roles: that of strategic planner and "enabler" and that of direct provider of housing advice services. From these two roles, four possible models of the role of local authorities can be distinguished:

A   Strategic planner and enabler; non-provider, with the voluntary sector seen as the provider, funded through contracts or grants;

B   Strategic planner and enabler; provider of "comprehensive" service (directly or by contracting with outside suppliers) with no role seen for the voluntary sector by the authority other than as contractor;

C   Strategic planner and enabler; provider of services to co-ordinate and complement voluntary and other providers (directly or by contracting out);

D No strategic role; *ad hoc* providing role possibly concentrated on homelessness and council tenancy issues; no view on the role of the voluntary sector.

9.19   Model C is the most attractive for voluntary agencies and the most effective for local authorities since it acknowledges the advantages as well as the inevitability of a range of provision in their area. Within this model, though, there is scope for great variation in overall advice provision, and in the relative roles of local authority and voluntary organisations. In practice the range of options for authorities in relation to direct provision extends from a small role (rather than no role) to a large role, with the voluntary sector playing a complementary or supplementary role in most areas, and in a few substituting for statutory provision through grants or contracts.

9.20   The other models are all, in different ways, unsatisfactory. Model D can be rejected, even though it describes the situation that exists where the strategic role has not been very well developed. Models B and C are seen by many authorities as the best options. But model B is unconvincing for two reasons. It fails to acknowledge the existence of voluntary sector provision, which will exist irrespective of the authority's attitude. And it fails to take account of the need for independent advice which is seen most clearly when a client is in dispute with the authority itself. Model A is also flawed since it fails to acknowledge the inevitability of the authority playing a role in aspects of advice provision, for example in its role as administrator of Housing Benefits, improvement grants and council house allocations policies.

9.21   There is great variety in the organisation and delivery of housing advice services in local government. All authorities employ staff in jobs which have an advice role, recognised as such to varying degrees. Examples include staff involved in community care, housing benefit administration, rent arrears recovery, improvement grants and the administration of the homelessness laws. The possible role of health workers, social workers and police officers also needs to be recognised.

9.22   If authorities wish to go beyond these duties and roles, to provide a wider identifiable housing advice service or centre, this can be organised in different ways:

–   a centre separate from the housing department;

–   a section or unit which is part of the housing department;

–   a service which is provided by staff whose remit is mainly or only to provide housing advice based in a section or unit with wider duties;

–   a service which is part of the remit of staff with other duties;

–   a service which is provided jointly in a partnership with another agency.

9.23   Where housing advice is closely associated in organisational terms with another part of the housing authority's work, the advice staff might be working alongside homelessness, needs, allocations, or private sector sections of housing departments, for example. Tenancy relations officers can work from a variety of organisational settings - housing advice services or centres, private sector sections, and environmental health departments.

9.24   Authorities with specialist advice services or centres need to decide whether to combine the administration of their homelessness duties with the provision of housing advice. In practice, some authorities feel that this is undesirable and the work of the centre would be dominated by the statutory homelessness duties; advice work inevitably receives less priority when numbers of applicants rises. In others, the advice service makes an initial assessment and refers applicants to the homelessness team only if it looks as though they may qualify for housing. Some authorities have created separate homelessness and advice services from previously combined units. Authorities with a housing advice centre, separately staffed, may use it as a reception point for any housing enquiries, with specialist staff drawn in as appropriate from homelessness, private sector or other units within the authority. Other authorities see similar benefits of convenience for clients in creating a network of local area offices.

Overall provision

9.25   In considering the present pattern of provision it is helpful to distinguish advice work that **supplements** statutory provision, that which **constitutes** or **substitutes** for statutory provision and that which **complements** it. Clarity about this will assist authorities in considering the contributions different agencies make, and the funding level they may wish to provide for them. Local authorities would then be in a position to make separate funding decisions about "statutory" and "voluntary" provision whichever agency or agencies are involved.

9.26   Few local authorities consider that their own specialist advisers can provide advice from information to advocacy in all situations. Voluntary organisations and most councils, supported by legal opinion, take the view that the advocacy role of local government officers must be limited where the client is in conflict with the council. Equally, though, it is hard to see that local authorities can have *no* role in housing advice provision, given their legal status in relation to, for example, landlord and tenancy issues, public health, improvement grants, and homelessness.

9.27   In general, many authorities demonstrate a pattern of voluntary and statutory provision *complementing* or *supplementing* each other, not always as the result of conscious design. Much less frequent is the voluntary sector *substituting* for statutory sector provision, although it is possible that a new duty on authorities to secure comprehensive advice provision will alter this pattern, especially where local authority services are least developed.

Who is served?

9.28   Housing advice services can be provided either for anyone who asks or for specific target groups. Target groups may be defined with reference to individual or family needs, or factors such as tenure, or with reference to area of residence. Voluntary organisations which provide housing advice as part of another role are more likely to target their services - to serve groups such as homeless people on the streets, young single people, or victims of domestic violence. In practice, in both the local authority and voluntary sectors, clients tend to be poor and vulnerable people, single people on low incomes, people with debts and other financial difficulties, and people with disadvantages which make it harder for them to operate in the private market.

9.29   Broadly, two models of access and delivery co-exist, often in the same agency. The dominant model is the reactive service responding to clients on request, and three types of access can be distinguished. Most common is the use of an *office base* which enquirers can visit or telephone for advice. The *telephone-only advice service* is growing in popularity, but few exist so far. The third form of access is *by referral*, which raises the issue of the links between agencies, and the arrangements for clients.

9.30   Reactive services operate on the implicit assumption that people seek out services when they need them. In contrast, proactive services attempt to reach people in advance of or in the midst of a housing crisis, or to publicise rights and obligations even though help has not been sought. Three types of proactive service illustrate the possible range. *Outreach work* delivers a service to an area or a client group which might not normally use a centre-based service; but such outreach services still must somehow convince people to take advantage of the advice available. *Education and training* services seek to increase the general level of knowledge of housing rights and obligations. *Promotional work* involves providing information about advice services, for example, advising landlords about their obligations even though no advice has been sought. Another example is the personal housing plans experiment funded by Scottish Homes,[3] in which individuals on the council waiting list are offered the opportunity to receive personal advice about options. There is a strong emphasis on preventative work in some proactive advice giving.

---

3.   Alexander, D. & McNicol, M. (1995) *Personal Housing Plans - A Technique. Report by Rural Forum, Scotland, for Skye & Lochalsh District Council*, Edinburgh, Homepoint, Scottish Homes.

9.31   There is no well-established method for assessing the need for housing advice services. Most agencies rely on measures of the demand for existing services, taking account of any apparent low take up by particular groups, such as ethnic minorities, or hostel residents. Gaps in provision can be identified from existing clients' needs, and from demographic, housing, economic or social conditions and developments. In some areas council tenants are seen as less well served, and in other areas they are seen as less needy, given their relatively secure, good quality housing.

Networks

9.32   The relationships between agencies is an important issue in the delivery and development of services. In considering the extent, nature and development of provision, therefore, local authorities and voluntary organisations should ensure mechanisms exist to promote contact and joint working between agencies operating at the local level. The likely benefits include:

- the identification of resources, needs and service gaps;

- sharing of specialist support services, including training;

- clarity about roles and referral and consultation mechanisms;

- improved joint planning;

- the development of new or joint services

9.33   What may appear to be a good organisational working relationship may depend on a relationship established between individual officers and so may be vulnerable to staff change, unless the right conditions exist for new staff also to establish good relations with others.

9.34   Networks can be developed, with support and assistance and trust between agencies. But in the early stage of developing a network individual agencies require to be approached sensitively since suggestions about establishing or improving networks may be taken as criticism of existing practice.

Local forums and joint projects

9.35   Three types of local forum can be detected. One brings together *workers*, the second brings together *organisations* and the third brings together both workers and organisations. These benefit from being convened and serviced using the resources of one of the agencies involved, sometimes the local authority. The focus may be "private sector" issues, or homelessness, or community care rather than housing advice services *per se*. Significant developments in advice services can arise from the work of such forums, and there seems to be no single formula for success.

9.36   Joint projects can be established at national or local level, as the NHAS illustrates (see 6.7). Sometimes these joint projects are difficult to categorise as statutory or voluntary. Some of the most innovative services involve creating a new structure such as a committee, for example, to bring together several agencies to provide a new service.

9.37   It is helpful to consider four different types of working arrangement separately, though in practice they may be conducted simultaneously:

- referral and consultation processes between agencies;

- relationships between 'specialist' and 'generalist' services;

- relationships between primary and secondary services;

- joint service provision, training and planning.

Referrals and consultations

9.38   People's housing problems do not necessarily manifest themselves in neat packages which allow agencies to specialise in assisting people. So referrals between agencies inevitably take place, and may be governed by formal agreements or less formal understandings about organisations' roles. Knowledge of the role and expertise of other agencies, through training, previous personal contact, or the production of directories of services will encourage staff to refer on when appropriate.

9.39   In both voluntary and local authority sectors an important distinction can be made between *referral* of clients to another agency, and *consultation*, where an agency might seek specialist advice, for example, from a law centre, in order to handle a case itself. A confusion between referral and consultation is evident in some cases, and may explain why some advice agencies are said to be particularly keen to "keep" their own clients - more positively, this may be an indicator of a model of service delivery in which one adviser remains the contact person throughout the history of the case, drawing on expertise as necessary from within or outside the agency, and, if appropriate, organising a case conference for relevant agencies. The extent and nature of referral and consultation needs to be mapped as a step in defining roles and ensuring clients are well served.

Relationships between "specialist" and "generalist" services

9.40   Three alternative types of relationship between specialist and generalist advice agencies can be distinguished: the hospital consultant/GP model, the network model and the one door model. In practice these are unlikely to exist in a pure form.

9.41   The first type was promoted by the National Consumer Council in 1977,[4] and is based on the traditional national health service model of general practitioners easily accessible at local level, backed up by specialist consultants who are accessible primarily through the "generalist" service. Although this model is still sometimes used as a prescription for the development of advice services, it is also apparent that it is no longer generally applicable. The reasons for this include the difficulty in distinguishing "specialist" from "generalist" advice agencies. For example, CABx are increasingly providing their own specialist services in the fields of employment, immigration, housing, money and legal advice. In any case, they are capable of dealing with many specialist housing or other problems even without the resources of a specialist, though that expertise is required sometimes. Also "specialist" services such as law centres and welfare rights services often wish to be widely accessible, and not just through referrals. Another problem is the absence or inaccessibility of the full network of generalist advice agencies which the model commends. For these reasons, the pattern of housing advice provision is more complicated than the GP/specialist consultant model suggests.

9.42   The second model is the notion of a network involving a number of agencies, some with specialist expertise, others without, some working at local level, some at regional or national level, and all linked so that they may tap into each others resources and refer clients to each other as appropriate. This model is implicit in the work started by HomePoint in Scotland towards accreditation of any private, public or voluntary agency which meets certain standards of provision. This could lead to the adoption of a logo which would become as familiar as the *"i"* used by tourist information offices, and would be encountered in high streets and public buildings throughout the country. This could be termed the *multiple, direct model* since it emphasises the possibility of establishing in the public's mind the wide range of possible sources of direct assistance on housing issues, and their accessibility. In practice, this model is poorly developed due to the relative absence of quality standards, and of liaison, communication and referral mechanisms in some cases.

9.43   The third model is the *one door model*, which has influenced the development of advice shops and arcades where a number of advice agencies are based, so easing access to the right agency. Once through this "door" the client is able to gain access to whatever specialist advice services are required, because agencies are co-operating in partnership with each other. This model bears some resemblance to the modern health centre where a patient may gain access to a doctor but also, if needed, a nurse, a counsellor, a health visitor and a range of other specialists.

---

4. National Consumer Council (1977) *The Fourth Right of Citizenship: A Review of Local Advice Services*, NCC.

Relationships between primary and secondary services

9.44   The distinction between primary (advice giving to clients) services, and secondary services which provide training, information and other support seems to be clearly understood by advice agencies, but in practice few organisations provide unambiguous examples of one or the other type of service. However, national federations such as NACAB, CHAR and FIAC are examples of organisations providing only secondary services, and such services are less likely to get drawn into primary advice work if they operate at regional or national level, or with very clear direction and management. An expansion in the extent of primary advice work would require an expansion or reorientation in the provision of secondary services, if quality were to be maintained.

9.45   Two models for funding secondary services can be compared: the statutory funding model and the fee income model. NACAB provides an example of government funding (supplemented from some other sources). The fee income model is illustrated by FIAC which struggles to survive on an income derived from membership fees, earnings from services such as training, and project income. Agencies such as Shelter provide services to their local groups but also to any organisation which is able to pay, for example, the fee for a training course.

Joint planning service provision

9.46   A useful distinction can be drawn between joint strategic planning and joint service provision, though in practice the two may be carried out simultaneously. Examples of the former appear to be less common, and include quarterly meetings between senior staff of a housing department and an independent housing aid centre to discuss overall provision and emerging issues. Joint service provision, such as a rota of statutory and voluntary agencies providing advice when repossession orders are being considered in court, may lead to collaboration in the development of a new project or organisation.

Resources

9.47   Different types of agency can bring different types of resource to housing advice work. All agencies need money, but some agencies have other resources such as volunteers' time and skills. Voluntary organisations can also offer independence, responsiveness and accessibility.

9.48   The sources of funding for local authority housing advice services are largely restricted to the local authority's own accounts, and these same local authority accounts are an important source of funding for voluntary organisations. Some central government funding for voluntary sector advice services has been particularly influential in developing new services, and the voluntary sector may also receive charitable donations as well as resources in kind.

9.49   For local authorities, models for funding advice services should follow from strategies for overall provision and roles. Funding is a particular focus of concern between the voluntary and statutory sectors, and, while reviews of roles and services are one way of attempting to achieve a rationale for funding decisions, they will not be a substitute for hard funding decisions. Local authorities have had two models for funding the voluntary sector: grants and contracts, of which the former has been dominant in practice. This is changing as authorities increasingly seek to demonstrate value for money and accountability through the introduction of service level agreements and, in a few cases so far, contracts.

9.50   The cost of housing advice services is very closely related to the cost of staff. The costs for some voluntary sector providers can be very low and are achieved by the use of volunteers. This makes them very vulnerable to funding cuts; but, more positively, it makes them very efficient at levering more service provision from a relatively low statutory funding level.

9.51   The introduction of a new statutory requirement for comprehensive housing advice services means that higher overall expenditure on advice may be required in some areas. The exact level of expenditure required cannot be quantified, but the need will be greatest, relatively, where present provision is least. Collaboration between the voluntary and local authority sectors over funding will provide the best prospects for maximising resources, even though some tensions will remain.

Monitoring and evaluation

9.52   Methods for evaluating the quality and value for money represented by advice services are poorly developed, partly reflecting the intrinsic difficulties involved. Measuring inputs (resources consumed) and throughput (cases handled) have dominated in evaluation because they are easier to measure than outputs or outcomes. Even when outcomes are measured, as in the practice of attributing to housing advice work a successful retention of a home or rehousing, there exists the possibility that factors other than housing advice (such as improved economic circumstances) were at work.

9.53   Some local authorities have developed models for calculating benefits which demonstrate that the cost of operating and staffing a housing advice service can be found from savings in the cost of temporary accommodation. There is scope to debate the methodology of such models, but there is no doubt that substantial financial and social costs can be saved. Local authority associations or the Chartered Institute of Housing might be appropriate forums in which to consider whether a model for use in all local authorities could be devised. Until this is achieved it may be misleading to claim that housing advice is cost effective in market efficiency terms. But even if it is not, the call on public - not necessarily housing - resources may be justified.

9.54   Whether evaluation takes place with reference to "process" issues, such as how the service is delivered, or "product" issues such as what the outcome is, there is a danger that the needs of those who do not use advice agencies are neglected. Too little is known about the general population's perception of the incidence of personal housing problems and what was done about them including who, if anyone, they contacted, and with what perceived results and satisfaction.

Performance indicators

9.55   Some advice services have grown haphazardly or in response to particular funding opportunities and may as a result have poorly developed monitoring and evaluation mechanisms. Other services, in the voluntary and local authority sectors, have created their own mechanisms or had them imposed. For example, some local authorities can set savings in the use of temporary accommodation as a result of housing advice intervention against costs, or use the number of homes saved as an indicator. Voluntary organisations in receipt of central government funds usually have a number of obligations placed on them to demonstrate value for money, largely through the use of indicators.

9.56   Monitoring and evaluation methods must be chosen to allow achievement of objectives to be measured. Given the multiplicity and complexity of most advice agencies' objectives, a simple system for monitoring and evaluation is unlikely to be sufficient. Each objective has different implications for monitoring, as Figure 9.2 shows for the four purposes of housing advice outlined in Chapter 3.

9.57   Some common strands as well as some differences are apparent in the indicators shown in Figure 9.2. The quality of advice provided, as measured by the advice agency, is a well-established focus of indicators, and is considered below, and attention is now focusing also on clients' assessments of the quality of services. The figure shows, however, the limitations of the most commonly used "indicator" of advice services - the number of enquiries handled.

9.58   No general conclusion about the effectiveness of housing advice services can be reached here, but increasingly agencies should be able to make their own statements about effectiveness, taking account of the adverse conditions of poverty, unemployment, poor health and vulnerability within which they and their clients work.

Figure 9.2	Evaluating achievements in housing advice
Objective	**Monitoring Emphasis**
Citizenship	- number of clients
	- accessibility of service
	- quality of advice offered
	- satisfaction of client with advice
Policy	- policy impacts detected
	- collation of statistics on problems
	- dissemination to policymakers
Service Rights	- outcome for client
	- quality of advice
	- satisfaction of client with housing
Market Efficiency	- outcome for client
	- outcome for housing stock use
	- cost effectiveness

Quality systems

9.59   Three models of "quality control" systems can be detected, and it is possible to operate more than one at a time. For the voluntary sector, however, there is some danger that funders may impose very complex monitoring frameworks, creating too onerous requirements for data collection.

9.60   The first model involves tying funds to conformity with quality standards. It is illustrated in the development of legal aid funding for advice agencies involving the adoption of conditions laid down by the Legal Aid Board (in a pilot funding exercise for non-solicitor advice agencies). The Legal Aid Board's requirements are very much concerned with "process" rather than "outcome" issues, and have imposed some additional administrative burdens on advice agencies. The benefits seen by advice agencies are the additional resources brought to advice work.

9.61   The second example of quality standards is the use of peer consensus amongst advisers themselves. For example, CHAS has developed a short Handbook of guidance for groups within the network. It is the result of a participative process involving staff and committee members and it has been accepted by all the local groups. There are no sanctions for non-compliance.

9.62   The third approach involves the adoption of standards set down by a lead agency. This is illustrated in Scotland, where the Scottish Homes Homepoint project has produced a standards and good practice manual[5], which is being marketed to anyone interested in adopting it voluntarily. It provides a much more comprehensive approach than the CHAS Manual, but the standards equally cannot be imposed on any agency. Both systems would be capable of development in the future in ways that might involve sanctions for non-compliance, such as withdrawal of accreditation or funding.

---

5.   Chariton (1995) *Housing Information And Advice Services National Standards And Good Practice Manual*, Edinburgh: Homepoint, Scottish Homes.

Staff and training

9.63 Advice work is labour intensive, and so the quality and training of staff is a key aspect of providing quality in service provision. This is appreciated as well in the voluntary as the local authority sector. However, there is some concern in the voluntary sector that the demands of quality systems may place an unreasonable burden of training and management responsibility on advice agencies which may suffer high rates of staff turnover and which rely to a large extent on the use of part-time volunteers.

9.64 The moves towards NVQs, a contract culture, and greater concern about public accountability combined with the introduction of a new statutory duty all point towards an increasingly managerial and professionalised service. A new statutory duty has often led to the creation of new professional groups sometimes together with new co-ordinating and monitoring arrangements, and housing advice work may develop in that way. Volunteer staffing may become increasingly rare. Advice workers may emerge more clearly as an occupational group, with a clearer view of what constitutes advice work, with recognised qualifications and with a more consistent ethos. Housing advice may become something that only experts can do, rather than something that almost anyone can do with minimal training. In this case a *professionalised* service would exist.

9.65 An alternative staffing model would place increased emphasis on volunteering, on the role of the voluntary sector, and on the cost effectiveness of grant aiding to assist the maximum use of volunteers and to ensure quality standards are reached. This *voluntary model* seems unlikely to be promoted though several voluntary agencies stressed the advantages of supplementing their contribution through the role of volunteers.

Service developments

9.66 A comprehensive housing advice service would aim to provide a full range of forms of advice over a wide range of housing issues to a wide range of clients. In some areas, therefore, there is a clear need for new services. In these areas, especially, local authorities and the voluntary sector will require to consider carefully how the statutory duty to secure comprehensive housing advice provision will be met. The voluntary sector, including specialist housing aid agencies which do not have a presence in an area, may be interested in assisting in ways which can build on existing resources.

9.67 In other areas, a more comprehensive service will be in place, but perhaps the local authority and the voluntary sector have identified gaps or weaknesses and difficulties. For example, there are client groups such as owner occupiers in mortgage difficulty and ethnic minority groups who are consistently identified as needing more advice. There is scope for more proactive and secondary advice service provision, and some primary agencies should devote more time to proactive and secondary work in order to try to avoid future crises, or to ensure that a wider range of professionals have the training to provide at least some housing advice. For all these difficulties and others there are examples of successful attempts to overcome them, and of service developments such as rent deposit schemes which provide access to housing that would not otherwise be available. The achievements of housing advice services require greater publicity so that they may be replicated and built on. This report is intended to assist that process.

Appendix: Research method

Stage 1: Initial review

A1.1   This appendix describes the methods used in the research on which this report is based. The study can be seen as having three stages, although in practice the second and third were carried out simultaneously.

A1.2   The first few weeks of the study were used to carry out a literature review, and interviews with key agencies involved in housing advice. Library searches demonstrated a scarcity of recent published material on housing advice services, but provided some useful historical material. Recent research and writing on specific housing policy issues contain some analysis of the operation of advice services particularly in relation to homelessness and community care. A small number of evaluations of advice services exist. More ephemeral material such as annual reports was collected from several of the agencies interviewed.

A1.3   A list of 19 national agencies was drawn up, encompassing major national housing advice agencies, local authority associations, and other national bodies. At local level five agencies were approached - a CAB in the Midlands, a local authority housing advice centre in the North, a specialist agency working with single homeless young people in London, a local authority with a network of generalist advice centres in the North East, and a federation of agencies involved in homelessness in South London. A total of 24 interviews were conducted. All who were approached agreed to be interviewed and interview times varied from one hour 15 minutes to three hours.

A1.4   At this stage an interim report was written, summarising findings, identifying issues and models of practice, and indicating some potential case studies. This provided assistance in framing the questionnaire surveys, and in identifying issues for examination in the case studies.

Stage 2: Surveys
Telephone survey of local authorities

A1.5   Stage 2 consisted of two surveys. First, a sample of one in three local authorities was selected for a telephone survey. The telephone method was chosen because it was likely to lead to a higher response rate than a postal survey, and it provided an opportunity to explore some of the issues in greater depth than a postal survey would have allowed. It proved particularly valuable in achieving an understanding of the complex organisational arrangements applying in some authorities for the delivery of advice services.

A1.6   The sample for the local authority survey was drawn at random from lists of each of four types of authority: inner and outer London boroughs; metropolitan councils; and district councils, stratified according to the level of housing pressure, as measured by the incidence of acceptances of applications for accommodation under Part III of the Housing Act 1985. Case study local authorities which did not appear in the first draw were added. The sample of district councils was checked to ensure representation of authorities which had transferred their housing stock to alternative landlords. The sample was weighted to ensure sufficient representation of London boroughs and metropolitan authorities to enable meaningful analysis of results. A reserve list of matching authorities was drawn in case of refusals.

A1.7   The sample was 128 authorities and the response was 106, a rate of 83 per cent. Officers, typically section heads, identified by Housing Directors as having some responsibility for housing advice were usually able to complete the interview in 45 minutes, although some interviews lasted up to one and a half hours. The sample and the response rates for each type of authority is shown in Table A1.1.

Table A1.1	Telephone survey of local authorities: sample and response rate			
	All England Population	Sample Number	Respondents	
			Number	%
London	6,929,078	24	23	96
Metropolitan	10,867,182	25	22	88
District	30,732,522	79	61	77
Total	48,528,782	128	105	83

Postal survey of voluntary organisations

A1.8 A sample of voluntary organisations in one in six local authority areas was drawn up for a postal survey. This sample was drawn by using contacts established during the initial review and during the telephone survey to construct lists for each of sixty local authority areas. The sixty were selected in a similar way to the selection of the local authorities for the telephone survey. Two types of voluntary organisation were included: advice agencies, and social welfare agencies which might be expected to give housing advice as part of a wider or more specialist role. All advice agencies were included, and so were voluntary organisations providing services to homeless people and to other vulnerable groups such as those entitled to community care services. Housing associations were included if they were known to provide advice services extending beyond their role as landlord.

A1.9 Questionnaires were sent to 445 organisations. A number were duplicated or returned by the Post Office, leaving 432. Of these, 38 were returned by organisations who said they did not provide housing advice services. It is likely there were additional non-respondents who did not provide housing advice, but it was impractical to establish that. The effective sample was 407, and the response was 148, a rate of 36%. The sample and response rate by type of area is shown in Table A1.2.

Table A1.2	Response to postal survey of voluntary organisations			
	Sent Out	Effective Sample Number*	Respondents	Effective Response Rate (%)
London	123	110	40	36
Metropolitan	207	193	54	28
District	114	104	54	52
Total	445	407	148	36

* not including voluntary organisations which do not provide housing advice.

A1.10 The relatively poor response rate was partly attributable to the fact that the survey was not carried out by telephone. It was also, some organisations said, due to their lack of time. Their staff were hard-pressed and found it difficult to give the hour that might be required to complete the questionnaire and find supporting papers to send with it. Only one organisation said it refused to complete the questionnaire because it saw no value in the research.

Stage 3: Case studies

A1.11 At the same time as proceeding with the surveys, a total of twenty case studies, of two types, were selected. The first type was made up of ten local authority areas which had come to attention as providing examples of particular models of service delivery and relationships with the voluntary sector. All ten local authorities agreed to co-operate, and in all cases the voluntary sector agencies contacted also agreed to take part. These case studies involved one or two visits of one or two days in which local authority and voluntary sector agencies were interviewed, sometimes interviews with clients or other meetings were observed, and other information, such as annual reports and policy statements, was collected.

A1.12 The second type of case study was intended to identify innovative projects, policy initiatives or organisations, within either the local authority or voluntary sector. Ten were identified, of which all but one organisation agreed to take part. The refusal came from a law centre which declined to take part due to staffing difficulties.

This report

A1.13 This report combines quantitative and qualitative data collected in the research to draw conclusions about the nature and extent of housing advice services in England. Data on some aspects of resources proved hard to collect, and a detailed consideration of consumers' views of advice services was beyond the scope of this project.